TRAINING
MENTORS
IS NOT ENOUGH

TRAINING MENTORS IS NOT ENOUGH

HAL PORTNER

CORWIN PRESS, INC.
A Sage Publications Company
2455 Teller Road
Thousand Oaks, CA 91320-2218

E-mail: order@corwinpress.com
Call: (800) 818-7243   Fax: (800) 4-1-SCHOOL
www.corwinpress.com

For information:

Corwin Press, Inc.
A Sage Publications Company
2455 Teller Road
Thousand Oaks, California 91320
E-mail: order@corwinpress.com

Sage Publications Ltd.
6 Bonhill Street
London EC2A 4PU
United Kingdom

Sage Publications India Pvt. Ltd.
M-32 Market
Greater Kailash I
New Delhi 110 048 India

Printed in the United States of America

Library of Congress Cataloging-in-Publication Data

Portner, Hal
    Training mentors is not enough: Everything else schools and districts need to do / by Hal Portner.
        p. cm.
    ISBN 0-7619-7737-6
    ISBN 0-7619-7738-4 (pbk.)
    1. Mentoring in education—United States. 2. First year teachers—United States. 3. Teachers—In-service training—United States. I. Title.
    LB1731.4 .P675 2001
    371.102—dc21

                                                                00-012349

This book is printed on acid-free paper.

01 02 03 04 05 06 10 9 8 7 6 5 4 3 2 1

Acquisitions Editor:	Robb Clouse
Corwin Editorial Assistant:	Kylee Liegl
Production Editors:	Nevair Kabakian/Denise Santoyo
Editorial Assistant:	Candice Crosetti
Typesetter:	Rebecca Evans
Cover Designers:	Tracy E. Miller/Michelle Lee

Contents

Preface   ix

Who Should Read This Book   x

Overview of the Contents   x

Acknowledgments   xi

About the Author   xiii

Introduction   1

The Inadequacy of Adequate   2

Programs and Systems   3

The Law of Unanticipated Consequences   4

LUC and Mind-Sets   5

One District's Metamorphosis From Adequate to Exemplary   6

Some Definitions   7

Exemplary Local Mentoring Support System: The Model   8

1. Commitment   11

Commitment = Beliefs + Expectations + Reward   12

Beliefs   12

    Exercise 1.1 Beliefs That Relate to Mentoring   14

Expectation of Success   15

Reward, or, What's in It for Me?   16

    Exercise 1.2 Identify Potentially Committed People   18

Build and Reinforce Commitment   19

    Exercise 1.3 Help Others to Commit   19

2. Putting Commitment to Work   22

Public Affirmation   23

The Planning and Implementation Committee:
    Its *Modus Operandi*   25

Committee Dynamics   25

    Exercise 2.1 What's Going On in Your Committee?   27

Group Decision Making   29

Beware the Illusion of Agreement   30

3. The Macrosystem   32

State Mandates, Guidelines, and Incentives   32

    Exercise 3.1 Who Is Your State Department
    of Education Contact? What Does Your State
    Require? Recommend? Fund?   35

Higher Education   35

    Exercise 3.2 How Colleges and Universities Can
    Help Your Program   37

Professional Associations and Organizations   39

    Exercise 3.3 Reinforce Professional Support   39

The Internal Macrosystem   40

    Exercise 3.4 Take Advantage of Change   41

    The Power of Culture and Tradition   42

    The Specter of Past Experience   44

4. Roles and Responsibilities (It Takes a Community to Induct a Teacher)   46

Administrators   47

Supervisors   49

Nonmentoring Veteran Teachers   49

Mentors   51

New Teachers (Mentees)   52

Mentoring Program Coordinator   52

    Exercise 4.1 What Others Can Do   53

5. Policies, Procedures, and Particulars   54

Time   55

Money   58

Exercise 5.1 Prioritize Budget Line Items 60

Compensation 62

Selection of Mentors 63

Mentor Training 65

Matching Mentors and Mentees 67

Monitoring 68

When to Intervene 69

Other Decisions to Contemplate 69

6. Professional Development for Newly Trained Mentors 71

Principles of Professional Development for Trained Mentors 72

Mentors Must Take Charge of Their Own Ongoing Professional Development 73

Look to MoM for Help 79

Manage Professional Development Time 80

7. Evaluating the Fledgling Mentoring Program 81

Why Evaluate? 82

Evaluating a New Program for Accountability 82

Exercise 7.1 Your Program's Baseline Data and Their Implications 84

Exercise 7.2 Develop an Outcome Through the Process of Reflection 86

Evaluating for Purposes of Improvement 89

Exercise 7.3 Respond to Areas of Concern 90

Collecting Data to Evaluate for Improvement 91

8. Some Other Programs Related to Mentoring 93

Support and Learning Groups for New Teachers 93

Co-Mentoring 95

Peer Assistance and Review 96

9. Inventing the Future: Planning an Exemplary Program 99

Turn Meeting Hours Into Action Minutes 99

Exercise 9.1 Action Minutes   100

Consider the Possibilities   101

Organize Your Plan   102

Exercise 9.2 Mentoring Program Planning Organizer   103

Planning Progress Checklist   105

Resource A: Professional Associations   **107**

References   **109**

Preface

I have searched high and low, but can't find anyone to bad-mouth the idea of assigning good, caring veteran teachers as mentors to new teachers. Mentoring new teachers is one of the hottest things going in education today. Mentoring is being touted as *the* way to launch new teachers into their careers and to reduce the probability of their leaving prematurely.

Experienced teachers helping induct beginning teachers into the profession is nothing new, of course. Years ago, if mentoring existed at all within the culture of a school, it probably took place as an informal response to a new teacher seeking help or assumed the form of assistance offered to a new teacher by a caring and experienced colleague. Over the past 30 years, however, the mentoring of new teachers in many districts has been less and less left to chance and become more of a formalized program featuring a variety of policies and procedures. In its 1999 publication *Creating a Teacher Mentoring Program*, the National Foundation for the Improvement of Education (NFIE) observes that "mentoring programs have become more structured, more formal, and more dependent on the cooperation and good offices of school administrators, teacher representatives, and higher education faculty." The NFIE publication goes on to cite Tom Ganser, director of field experiences at the University of Wisconsin–Whitewater, who asserts that mentoring programs have shifted from "first-generation" to "second-generation," and that second-generation programs are:

> more likely [than the earlier ones] to *require* participation by new teachers; extend for periods longer than one year; match protégés with a number of mentors who provide assistance in different areas of expertise; attend more closely to the systemic issues that influence the effectiveness of new teachers; and abide by clear, written agreements, often between a school district and its teacher association.

Teacher mentoring programs, formal and informal, have been around for at least a generation. Educators have known or suspected all along—and research and experience have proven them to be right—that support of new teachers in the form of mentoring by seasoned peers not only contributes to the induction and retention of novices into the profession, but also provides a positive professional experience for the veteran teachers who do the mentoring.

Today, mentoring is no longer considered an option. The education establishment has made mentoring its premier modality for inducting, retaining, and developing new teachers.

Who Should Read This Book

I have written this book for educational leaders who want to develop an exemplary mentoring program or upgrade an existing one. It is for everyone committed to being part of a program that validates, supports, and celebrates every aspect of the mentor-mentee relationship. It is intended as (a) a how-to guide and workbook for planners and doers, (b) a practical reference and management tool for mentor program coordinators and members of program committees, and (c) a supplementary text for seminars or a graduate-level course in educational leadership or program development.

Overview of the Contents

The purpose of *Training Mentors Is Not Enough* is to help the reader (a) obtain broad-based commitment and participation from key individuals and groups; (b) understand and work within the larger environment in which a mentoring program operates; (c) form a mentoring committee and develop its capacity to make decisions effectively; and (d) support the program with pragmatic and effective policies, procedures, and resources.

The book consists of an introduction and nine chapters. The introduction presents mentoring as a valued component of contemporary educational philosophy and practice, differentiates between adequate and exemplary mentoring programs, and argues for the use of a systems mindset while developing and operating a program.

The nine chapters—each focusing on a key element essential to the viability of an exemplary program—offer down-to-earth discussions supplemented by anecdotes, commentary, examples, and interactive exercises designed to help the reader develop practical strategies appropriate to the culture and circumstances of his or her particular school or district.

The first chapter, *Commitment*, suggests how to identify and engage people and organizations that are committed to the belief that mentoring is a powerful way to develop and retain new teachers.

Chapter 2, *Putting Commitment to Work*, advocates a planning and implementation committee, describes the process of collaborative decision making, and pays attention to the group dynamics within which a committee operates.

Chapter 3, *The Macrosystem*, discusses the environment, the system of systems, within which the mentoring program operates. It looks at organizations, agencies, and programs both inside and outside the local district, and how these entities relate to a local mentoring program.

Chapter 4, *Roles and Responsibilities (It Takes a Community to Induct a Teacher)*, details ways in which a variety of people in a local education community can contribute to the development of a new teacher.

Chapter 5, *Policies, Procedures, and Particulars*, specifies the kinds of decisions a mentoring committee needs to make, and a variety of ways the results of those decisions might be implemented.

Chapter 6, *Professional Development for Newly Trained Mentors*, recognizes that newly trained mentors, like newly certified teachers, may have acquired skills and understandings but may not be able to apply them effectively in authentic settings. A variety of strategies and activities are suggested to address the need of newly trained mentors to enhance and expand their effectiveness.

Chapter 7, *Evaluating the Fledgling Mentoring Program*, provides ways to evaluate new or revised programs for purposes of both accountability and improvement.

Chapter 8, *Some Other Programs Related to Mentoring*, discusses three recently developed models—support and learning groups for new teachers, co-mentoring between and among experienced peers, and peer assistance and review for teachers who receive unsatisfactory evaluations—and examines their potential as components of a mentoring program.

Chapter 9, *Inventing the Future: Planning an Exemplary Program*, looks at each element of a mentoring program that a planning committee might want to incorporate, and guides the reader through the steps involved in the element's development and implementation.

After reading this book and working through its exercises, you will have gained a comprehensive perspective on what constitutes an exemplary mentoring program, and will have developed a variety of practical strategies for planning, implementing, managing, and nurturing such a program in your school or district.

Acknowledgments

It is with a great deal of gratitude and appreciation that I acknowledge the time, energy, and considerable expertise the following colleagues devoted to the critical review of this manuscript. Their comments and suggestions were most appropriate, and many were incorporated into the final version: William Allen, Superintendent of Schools, North Andover, Massachusetts;

Vincent L. Ferrandino, Executive Director, National Association of Elementary School Principals; Thomas Ganser, Director of Field Experiences, University of Wisconsin–Whitewater; Charles E. Gorban, Chair, Professional Development Council, Massachusetts Teachers Association; Frank Llamas, Coordinator, Southeast (MA) Tech Prep Consortium; and Carl O'Connell, Mentor Program Coordinator, Rochester (NY) Public Schools. Elaine Cantrell, an elementary principal in Sierra Vista, Arizona; Thomas Puccio, Principal, Malden (Massachusetts) Catholic High School; Pete Reed, Associate Director, Leadership Assessment and Development, National Association of Secondary School Principals; Shauna Shoptaw, a mentor teacher in a California school district; and Becky Sutusky, Dorchester School District Two, Summerville, South Carolina; are only a few of the many educators who have shared thoughts, insights, and materials that have influenced some of my writing in this book. Thank you, all.

I especially wish to thank Robert Pauker, educational consultant and cherished friend, for his astute advice and sincere encouragement.

My most profound thanks to my wife, Mary. This book would not have been written without her unflagging support and insightful feedback.

—*Hal M. Portner*
Northampton, Massachusetts

Photo by Walter Massa.

About the Author

Hal Portner is an experienced K–12 teacher and administrator. He was Assistant Director of the SummerMath Program for High School Women and Teachers, Mount Holyoke College, and for 14 years was a teacher and administrator in a Connecticut public school district. Portner holds a M.Ed. from the University of Michigan, a sixth-year Certificate of Advanced Graduate Study (CAGS) in Education Administration from the University of Connecticut, and for three years was with the University of Massachusetts Ed.D. Educational Leadership Program.

From 1985 to 1995, he was on the staff of the Connecticut State Department of Education, Bureau of Certification and Professional Development. While there he served as coordinator of the Connecticut Institute for Teaching and Learning and worked closely with school districts to develop and carry out professional development and teacher evaluation plans and programs. Among the major accomplishments of the bureau was the development, implementation, and fine-tuning of Connecticut's Beginning Educator Support and Training (BEST) program, a nationally acclaimed beginning teacher mentoring and assessment initiative.

Portner writes, consults, develops materials, and trains mentors for school districts and other educational organizations and institutions. He is the author of *Mentoring New Teachers* (1998), available from Corwin Press.

Please feel free to contact the author with feedback, suggestions, questions, anecdotes about mentoring, or just to say, "Hello." He can be reached by e-mail at Portner_Associates@CompuServe.com.

Introduction

I train experienced teachers to be mentors of new teachers. For the most part, these teachers volunteer to be mentors and to participate in mentor training. Typically, they look forward to the opportunity to help induct their new colleagues into the profession, and are eager to take on the responsibility of passing their expertise on to the next generation.

Although many of the districts with which I work have developed excellent mentoring programs, others have programs that they consider to be adequate, but which are actually jury-rigged efforts limited to training veteran teachers who have expressed interest in being mentors, and then assigning them to work with new teachers. Teachers and administrators from districts such as these often express frustration with their program, and hint at the need for something more—something beyond mentor training. When I ask what that *something* might be, the common answer is, "More structure."

I decided to find out what that elusive *something*—that "more structure"—might be, so I spent the past year reading the literature and communicating with teachers and administrators. I interacted with them face-to-face; during telephone conversations; via e-mail, Internet listservs, and chat rooms; and through the administration of written surveys. I listened to their anecdotes and insights. I eavesdropped as they reflected on data from research. In almost every instance the same assertions emerged: These educators understood and appreciated the value of mentoring, generally felt good about being mentors, and reported that they benefited greatly from the training and experience . . . *but* along with these positive perceptions there surfaced time and time again an undercurrent of concern, suspicion, and frustration.

From teachers, I heard, "Where do I find time to mentor? There's too much to do already. How will I be compensated? Since others consider mentoring the new teacher as my job, no one else wants to help her. I can't afford to be away from my classroom so often."

From administrators, "We have no choices; we are driven by state mandates. We don't have a budget to support a mentoring program. Our mentors are creative professionals. . . . They don't need my help. My parents want their child's teacher in the classroom teaching."

Of course, a number of schools and districts have created a climate and structure in which effective mentoring does take place and where there is no undercurrent of concern, suspicion, and frustration. Characteristically, these exemplary schools and districts place a high priority on the induction, support, and retention of their new teachers. They are energized by tangible commitments and guided by dedicated involvement from various constituents within the education community. They have developed and maintained a structure that takes into account such issues as time for mentoring, criteria for selecting mentors and matching them with mentees, incentives and compensation, and assessment of program effectiveness. They provide, maintain, and make accessible a comprehensive bank of resources to inform and support the program.

Everything I heard, read, and experienced, however, told me that developing and supporting such an exemplary mentoring program is easier said than done; that when we try to expand or modify an existing program or add another educational imperative—no matter how important or potentially beneficial—to our already overextended educational system, it is in danger of becoming a relatively ineffective, perfunctory exercise, unless

1. It is tailored to the specific culture and beliefs of the local district and its schools

2. It is built upon a broad base of commitment and participation from all stakeholders

3. It is designed, implemented, managed, assessed, and nurtured within a formal structure of collaborative problem solving and decision making

4. It receives ongoing support and resources, including provision for the ongoing professional development of its people

Together, these four components make up the mentoring support system that differentiates exemplary programs from adequate ones.

The Inadequacy of Adequate

Adequate mentoring programs more or less meet modest goals and are supported by minimum resources, but they neither operate systematically nor embody other elements that are essential to the ongoing success of mentoring programs. Characteristically, schools and districts with adequate mentoring programs have developed them around limited local commitment. For example, they tend to operate within a structure all too often adopted from an outside "model" and imposed on their local framework. They generally do not assess their programs. Even when they do attempt to assess, they are not likely to have a mechanism in place by which to analyze and reflect on the results or to make necessary modifications. Typically, these schools and districts have adopted adequate policies and procedures from other adequate programs, produced and distributed adequate memos and directives, and expect people to follow those directives . . . adequately. These districts may hope for superlative results from mediocre efforts, but in the long run they have settled for adequacy.

At this juncture, I would like to share with you an example of the kind of experience I've had with adequate mentoring programs that have prompted me to write this book.

Hilldale (not the district's real name) had an adequate mentoring program. Michelle was hired as the new and only art teacher in Hilldale's Westside Elementary School. The mentoring program's policy was to match new teachers with mentors from the same school, and, if possible, both mentor and mentee should be teaching the same grade and/or the same subject area.

Michelle taught students in grades 1 through 5. None of the other teachers in Michelle's school felt competent enough to mentor an art teacher, and regretfully declined the challenge. The school's principal considered mentoring important, so she asked Beverly, the art teacher from Eastside Elementary in Hilldale, to be Michelle's mentor. Beverly agreed. The combination of Beverly's and Michelle's schedules, along with the 5-mile distance between their schools, however, resulted in infrequent meetings between the two, and even those were possible only outside of school time. Consequently, the two teachers were not able to observe each other's classes—a vital mentoring procedure. They considered videotaping their classes, but never did. Although Michelle and Beverly were reimbursed for travel expenses, they felt that they should be compensated for the additional time spent after school, even though they were told that the budget didn't allow for such an expense. For all practical purposes, Michelle didn't have a mentor.

Programs and Systems

Mentoring operates best within a program. A mentoring program operates best within a system.

A *program* is a plan of things to be done or to take place, usually in sequence or chronological order. Agendas, calendars, schedules, and timetables are examples of programs. This is more than a definition; it is a mind-set. It implies checklist and lockstep. It suggests, "First you do this, then you do that." There is nothing wrong with a *program*. In fact, the concept is useful—even necessary—in carrying out the various aspects of mentoring. Selecting and matching mentors and mentees, arranging for mentor training, and devising forms to document the time mentors spend with mentees are examples of programmatic activities.

When we operate a mentoring program within a *system,* we think holistically. We are aware of patterns and relationships, and understand that everything we do in one area of a system affects the others—that when we change one thing, something else changes.

Within a systems mind-set, time ceases to be linear. Since all components are interconnected, when one part changes, the other parts will change at the same time. For instance, in the Hilldale scenario above, when the principal changed a procedure and went outside of her building to recruit a mentor for her new art teacher, there were immediate implications for adjustments in budget, contract language, schedules, decision-making protocol, mentor-mentee matching policy, and mentor training.

Perceiving and analyzing in terms of systems is not innate to most humans. According to Clinton J. Andrews and Carl Henn, who cochaired a workshop titled "Systems Thinking, Academic Standards, and Teacher Preparation" at Princeton University on April 5, 1997, "We are born blind to systems in three principle [sic] ways. We have an inherent inability to clearly perceive ourselves in (a) space, (b) in time, and (c) in our relationships to what appear to be remote objects, forces, people and events." Andrews and Henn go on to suggest that spatial blindness can keep us from grasping "big picture" connections; temporal blindness can keep us from planning for the unpredictable; and relationship blindness can lead to "one-step thinking," resulting in overly simplistic solutions that usually replace old problems with new ones. I would add that ignoring a systems approach is like riding a surfboard: The surfer isn't as interested in where the board is going as in keeping on top of things.

The Law of Unanticipated Consequences

Although mentoring new teachers has been hovering on the periphery of educational practice for some time, it was the result of a series of serendipitous cause-and-effect events, or what I like to call the *Law of Unanticipated Consequences* (LUC), that pushed mentoring into the center ring.

Among the most compelling situations that brought mentoring to the attention of educators was the realization, emphasized by President Clinton in his *Call to Action for American Education in the 21st Century,* that more new teachers than usual—nationally, about 2.2 million—would be needed over the next 10 years. Through hindsight, we can see that the growing need for more teachers was in turn the unanticipated consequence of

- Growing student enrollments (a.k.a. baby boomer echoes)
- Research supporting smaller student-teacher ratios in the classroom
- Proliferation of contractual limits on work loads

- The luring away of potential teachers by businesses offering higher salaries to college graduates
- The graying of the existing teacher pool
- Early retirement incentives offered as a way to save money and to infuse new blood into the profession

Another element was added to the mix in July 1997 with the publication of *The Seven Priorities of the U.S. Department of Education.* One of the areas stressed in that document was the need for "special efforts to retain beginning teachers in their first few years of teaching, because we now lose 30% due to a lack of support." Later in the same year, President Clinton issued his *Call to Action for American Education in the 21st Century,* in which he pointed out that one of the best special efforts school districts can make regarding new teacher retention was to "make sure that beginning teachers get support and mentoring from experienced teachers."

Soon thereafter, we began to experience another phase in the blossoming of teacher mentoring programs: Federal and state departments of education pumped money and data into their development and implementation. States passed laws—more than half the states in the United States require mentoring of some sort for entry-level teachers—and formulated regulations, developed guidelines, ran conferences and workshops, and awarded grants, all geared toward encouraging and supporting the mentoring of new teachers.

Professional associations and organizations, too, began to pay more attention to teacher mentoring issues. The Association for Supervision and Curriculum Development (ASCD), the National Association of Secondary School Principals (NASSP), the National Association of Elementary School Principals (NAESP), the National Staff Development Council (NSDC), the National Education Association (NEA), and the American Federation of Teachers (AFT), among others, produced a variety of thoughtful and insightful articles, policy statements, training materials, and conferences having to do with various aspect of the induction and mentoring of new teachers.

Teacher preparation programs added their leadership to the field of new teacher mentoring by reconfiguring student-teaching procedures, adding or modifying courses, conducting action research, and partnering with public schools and state education departments. Some of higher education's leading thinkers, researchers, and practitioners have added a great deal to our understanding about mentoring and its application.

LUC and Mind-Sets

Those who develop and operate mentoring programs will find themselves subject to LUC. There is, however, a fundamental difference between the way LUC operates in a program and in a system. This is because in a program, we react; in a system, we proact.

When we think with a *program* mind-set, change is considered primarily in terms of its effect on the component in which it occurs, and our efforts are directed toward dealing with that change. Later, when the echoes of that change affect still other components, we start all over again and deal with those situations. Using a *systems* mind-set, however, we anticipate that there will be unanticipated consequences. We expect change in one area to create simultaneous ripples in the others. Therefore, even though we may not fully know the nature of the impending change, we can prepare to deal with the "gestalt of change" rather than react to first one problem, then another.

For example, suppose a board of education votes to implement a world language program in two elementary schools, and directs the superintendent to hire one new foreign language teacher to service both buildings. A program-thinking mentoring committee would determine which trained mentor to assign to the new person, or perhaps which experienced teacher to recruit and train as a new mentor. A systems-thinking committee might do the same, but in addition would consider implications the board's action might have on the program's other components. They may, for example, ask, "Will our budget handle additional training and another stipend?" "Will we need to modify our mentor-mentee matching policies, because there are no experienced elementary foreign language teachers and the new person will be teaching in two buildings?" and "What mentoring resources might be available from foreign language teachers associations?"

One District's Metamorphosis
From Adequate to Exemplary

Midville's mentoring program had deteriorated a couple of years ago (this fictional district's story is a composite of several actual cases). During its active period, a few veteran teachers were asked each year to volunteer as mentors. Those who volunteered received some training and joined an existing pool of other mentors. Both new teachers and seasoned veterans could, on a voluntary basis, pair up with a mentor from this pool. Midville had an adequate mentoring program for interested novices and experienced teachers.

Then something changed. The state instituted a mandatory student testing program. Midville's students performed poorly on these achievement tests—well below state averages. The Midville school board made the improvement of state test scores a top priority. To their credit, they were wise enough to realize that this would take time and additional resources. They demanded top-to-bottom accountability, upgrading of curriculum and instruction, and a reassessment of several programs, including mentoring.

The district's administrative team instituted three changes in the mentoring program: (a) *all* new teachers will be assigned mentors; (b) mentors will schedule and document all meetings with their mentees; and (c) supervisors will receive written reports of mentees' progress, particularly in their ability to teach the curriculum areas being assessed in the statewide achievement tests.

Time for the Law of Unanticipated Consequences again. LUC manifested itself in Midville with a vengeance. The teachers' association claimed that treating employees differently— that is, *requiring* beginning teachers to be mentored and not others—was not only a negotiable issue, but also differentiated between teachers based on experience, and therefore was in violation of existing contract language. The teachers' association also charged that by requiring teachers to document dates and times of meetings, they were, *de facto*, being required to work extra time without extra pay. Furthermore, the association claimed that by requiring the submission of written reports, mentoring had become part of teacher evaluation. There was no joy in Midville; the mentoring program had struck out.

It took two years for the contesting parties even to consider the reinstitution of mentoring. It was finally agreed to hire a consultant to resurrect the mentoring program and to build into it a way to make changes without disrupting the program's effectiveness. The consultant, Ann Jefferies, started by recruiting a representative team from among school board members, administrators, and leaders of the teachers' association. After much discussion and negotiation, the team and then the education community at large eventually agreed that, yes, mentoring new teachers was a worthwhile endeavor.

Then Ann introduced the concept of systems thinking. The team looked through a "systems lens" at Midville's professional agreements and contracts; reviewed its policies on accountability, the budgeting process, teacher evaluation, and curriculum; and considered the implications imposed by these factors on new teacher induction and support. Then the committee designed its own systems of governance, structure, and resources, and built in mechanisms regularly to identify and accommodate inevitable change. Every committee member overtly supported the new design, which, among other things, provided for collaborative rather than unilateral decision making on major policy issues. Two years later, Midville was able to boast that it had an exemplary mentoring program.

Some Definitions

It will be helpful, as you read through the rest of this book and work through its exercises, to have an understanding of what I mean by certain terms. I have already introduced the idea of the *Law of Unanticipated Consequences*, and discussed my concepts of the terms *program*, *system*, and *adequate.* In the chapters that follow, I hope to clarify what I mean by *commitment, participation, structure,* and *program evaluation.*

There are other terms I use throughout this book that may have ambiguous meanings. This is how I define them.

Mentee: An educator—usually a novice teacher, but the term also refers to an experienced teacher new to an assignment, school, or district—who is the protégé of a mentor. Some districts, when referring to a mentee, use the terms *intern, inductee,* or *probationary teacher.*

Self-reliant teacher: A teacher who is willing and able (a) to generate and choose purposefully from among viable alternatives, (b) to act upon those choices, (c) to monitor and reflect upon the consequences of applying those choices, and (d) to modify and adjust in order to enhance student learning.

Mentor: An experienced educator who is willing and able to help a mentee become a self-reliant teacher. A mentor is *not* involved in decisions about rehiring, tenure, certification, or any other activity having to do with teacher evaluation, although he or she may help a mentee prepare for a formal evaluation.

Mentoring: The behaviors of a mentor that help his or her mentee become self-reliant. These behaviors include (a) building and maintaining relationships with mentees based on mutual trust, respect, confidentially, and professionalism; (b) gathering, diagnosing, and using data about mentees' ways of teaching and learning; (c) coaching mentees in ways that help them fine-tune their professional skills, enhance their grasp of subject matter, understand how students learn, locate, and use resources and expand their repertoire of teaching modalities; and (d) weaning mentees away from dependence by guiding them through the process of reflecting on decisions and actions for themselves, and by encouraging them to construct their own informed teaching and learning approaches.

Macrosystem: The nonmentoring environment—the system-of-systems—that surrounds a mentoring program; the various agencies, communities, cultures, beliefs, and other educational and organizational entities and patterns within which the local mentoring program operates.

School/district: Either an individual school or an entire school district, whichever applies to the reader's situation.

Exemplary Local Mentoring Support System: The Model

An exemplary local mentoring support system is composed of four interrelated parts. It is important to keep in mind that, because a local mentoring program is a system, when one component changes, they all change. The four elements are

1. A broad-based commitment and participation from key individuals and groups
2. A compatible relationship with the macrosystem within which the mentoring program operates
3. A viable structure—consistent with local mores—for problem solving, decision making, implementation, and program assessment
4. A comprehensive and accessible body of resources

As you can see, there are quite a few things beyond training mentors that are involved in the support of the mentoring relationship. For example, in addition to operating within a systems mind-set, a mentoring support effort requires (a) provisions for the active participation of committed people and key organizations; (b) strong and visible statements from the district or school and its professional associations that they value mentoring and consider it to be of high priority; (c) a set of written and accessible policies and procedures, collaboratively developed, that structure all aspects of the program, including its ongoing assessment and adjustment; and (d) available and accessible resources (time, money, staff, material, and equipment) to support the program's structure and future development. Without at least some elements from each of these, a program will be, at best, . . . adequate.

The chapters that follow will provide you and other planners and doers in your school or district with understandings, strategies, and tools designed to enhance your existing mentoring program if you already have one, or to establish and nurture an exemplary program if you do not.

1

Commitment

Two of the top-rated television shows of the 90s were the sitcom *Seinfeld* and the drama *ER*. Those of us who tuned in to these two programs on a regular basis got to know the personality and temperament of the characters we watched week after week.

Consider Seinfeld's friend, George Costanza, for example. We could always count on George when it came to how he handled relationships—like the time he fell in love with a woman in prison. This was an ideal situation as far as George was concerned; after all, by its very nature, their love affair placed few demands on him, which was just the way George liked his relationships to be. Therefore, it was no mystery to regular viewers why, as a character witness at her parole hearing, George gave testimony that was aimed at keeping the woman in jail. We laughed but were not surprised when his involvement with the woman ended after she finally did manage to get out of jail.

Carol Hathaway, the multifaceted emergency room head nurse in *ER*, had relationships, too—some transitory, others longer-lasting, all caring. Viewers could always count on the durability of one relationship in particular: the one she had with her job in the hospital's emergency room. In one segment, Carol was suspended for accidentally hooking up the wrong blood type to a patient, who died as a result. Over the next few episodes, Carol worked through her dishonor and guilt, and bravely faced the consequences. She persisted, however, in her efforts to resume her involvement as part of the emergency room's staff because, as she phrased it to one of her coworkers while still under suspension, "I've missed it here. I love my job."

Both George and Carol were involved in their relationships, but Carol was also committed. What does it mean to be committed? How is it different from being involved? Someone once graphically explained the difference this way: In a ham and egg breakfast, the chicken is involved; the pig is committed. I don't intend for you to go that far, but I will venture this: Without commitment, a district's relationship with a mentoring program will be adequate at best, probably short-lived, and over time hard-pressed to justify its existence.

This chapter examines the importance of commitment to the systemic support of a local mentoring program. It will help you determine your own personal commitment and suggest to you who else in your school or district might be committed to the support of a mentoring program. We will also consider what organizations and groups will need to commit to the program if it is to excel. Furthermore, the chapter will suggest ways to developed and enhance commitment over time. First, however, just what is commitment?

Commitment = Beliefs + Expectations + Reward

The resonance of the mentoring program with one's beliefs and values, confidence that one's efforts will result in the program's success, and the feeling that participation in the program addresses one's basic needs: These are the elements that add up to commitment. All three factors in the equation must be in operation in order for genuine commitment to exist.

Commitment is contagious. A few committed people can inspire commitment in others—not just by enthusiasm and example, but also by (a) suggesting to others how mentoring relates to their values and beliefs, (b) conveying expectations of the program's success, and (c) helping others realize how involvement in a mentoring program can advance their own professional and organizational agendas. Let's examine each of these factors in detail.

Beliefs

When we are doing something we believe in—when what we are doing sits well with our set of values and is relevant to our lives—we do it better; we do it with passion. This is why resonance with beliefs is part of the commitment equation. If we want to increase commitment in people, we need to help them see how supporting a mentoring program can also support their beliefs and values, both as individuals and as members of organizations.

Let's start with the assumption that anyone in your school, district, or community who is seriously interested in and knowledgeable about education believes that *the cornerstone of quality education in our schools is what happens between the teacher and the student* and that *high-quality teaching leads to high student achievement.*

If your school or district is like most, many of the teachers hired over the next few years will be new to the profession. It is generally conceded that many of these beginning teachers will not be fully prepared to handle the tasks they will face during the first weeks and months on the job. The common belief is that a beginning teacher is more likely to grow professionally—and to remain in the profession longer—if she or he interacts on a regular basis with a seasoned colleague: a mentor. This is borne out by the results of several research efforts, including a 1999 poll conducted by Recruiting New Teachers, an organization based in Belmont, Massachusetts. This poll showed that 91% of the general public approves of mentoring programs and believes mentoring is a worthwhile way to provide professional support to new teachers. You can help people connect their beliefs to mentoring by sharing this kind of information with them.

For example, here is the way John M., the president of a local teacher's association, communicated connections between beliefs and mentoring to the association's members. When John wrote his annual "Welcome back" memo to the association's members in September, he included a brief introduction of each of the district's five newly hired teachers. Below is the paragraph from John's memo that followed those introductions.

> Christine, Edward, Leroy, Shana, and Morgan are looking forward to joining us in providing our district's most precious resource— its children—with the high quality of educational experience that can only take place between a student and an exemplary teacher. During their first few weeks and months here, these new teachers will be looking to us—their experienced colleagues who know and appreciate the value of excellent teaching—for guidance and encouragement as they acclimate to our district's culture and seek to grow in their new roles and responsibilities as teachers. I know we won't let them down.

Exercise 1.1 Beliefs That Relate to Mentoring

This two-part exercise will help you get a sense of how your own personal beliefs about education might relate to mentoring. Once you "know thyself" in this respect, you will have a better understanding of why others may value mentoring.

First, what are three beliefs you hold most strongly about education? For example, I believe that education is more that learning facts: It is also about being willing and able to know what it is you need to know, why you need to know it, where and how to find it, what to do with it when you have it, and how to know to what extent it satisfied your need to know it in the first place.

Write your beliefs below.

1. _____

_____

2. _____

_____

3. _____

_____

Now, reflect on what you understand mentoring to be and how that understanding resonates with any or all of your beliefs about education.

For example, I agree with Ben Ward, a professor at Western Carolina University, who describes a novice teacher as having a simplistic concept of what teaching and learning is all about. The novice is likely to consider teaching to be mainly a matter of presenting information, while assuming that learning is largely—if not entirely—the students' responsibility. The novice works from the assumption that "I teach, you learn." A master teacher, on the other hand, assumes that "as a teacher, I see my role not merely as presenting information, but also as creating conditions that encourage students to learn and to be responsible for their own learning."

If left to their own devices, as is often the case, novice teachers may take years to reach the master teacher stage—if they ever do. The primary role of the mentor is to guide, encourage, and expedite the new teacher's journey toward becoming a self-reliant master teacher.

Write your reflections below.

_____

_____

_____

Expectation of Success

It must be difficult for Scott Adams's cartoon character Dilbert to feel committed to his company when, as he laments "I'm stuck in an assignment that has no hope of succeeding."[1] With the possible exception of a person who has faith that his or her school system will put together an exemplary mentoring program despite all odds, most people, like Dilbert, will need to have tangible reasons to feel confident that their efforts will succeed.

One way to engender confidence in the eventual success of a developing mentoring program is to provide the opportunity for potentially committed people to "get their feet wet"—to participate directly in the problem-solving, decision-making, and implementation aspects of designing and maintaining a local mentoring program. Chapter 2, "Putting Commitment to Work," discusses in detail the nature of such participation by committed—or at least very interested—people like yourself.

Another way to raise people's expectations for success is to share with them some of the research on and anecdotal material about the successful impact of mentoring. For example,

- *Mentored teachers remain in the profession longer.* Of 100 beginning teachers who were mentored in the University of Alabama's First-Year Teacher Pilot Program, 96% taught for a second year. Of the 100 beginning teachers in a nonmentored control group in the same study, only 80% returned for another year.

- *Mentored teachers are more self-reliant and successful teachers.* The Southwest Regional Laboratory demonstrated that beginning teachers in California who have participated in mentoring programs were, when compared to other beginning teachers who have not been mentored, more likely to (a) use instructional practices that improve student achievement, (b) assign challenging work to diverse student populations, (c) use new state curriculum frameworks, and (d) accomplish the goals of the curriculum. The California study also demonstrated that the benefits of induction programs correlated directly with their intensity: The more the programs provided, the greater their success.

- *Mentored teachers develop more quickly.* In her 1999 report *Solving the Dilemmas of Teacher Supply, Demands and Standards,* Linda Darling-Hammond writes that "beginning teachers who have access to intensive mentoring by expert colleagues . . . not only stay in the profession at higher rates but become competent more quickly than those who must learn by trial and error."

- *Mentoring supports supervision.* Since 1986, the Columbus, Ohio, and Rochester, New York, mentoring programs have reduced by nearly 50% the number of teachers who require remedial intervention.

- *Mentored teachers recognize the benefits of the program.* In its January 1999 report *Teacher Quality*, the National Center for Education Statistics reports that 7 out of every 10 teachers who receive mentoring at least once a week believe that their instructional skills have improved "a lot" as a result.

- *Experienced teachers grow professionally as a result of mentoring.* Many veteran teachers who mentor report that they experience substantial improvements to their practice as a result. As one teacher in Arizona put it, "All of us who were mentors changed radically. Our classroom management skills changed and improved. The way we related to other teachers in our area changed and improved. The skills that we used to work with students in our classroom changed and improved."

Reward, or, What's in It for Me?

The third criterion for commitment is the satisfaction of a need. The 1999 National Foundation for the Improvement of Education (NFIE) report *Creating a Teacher Mentoring Program* points out how successful mentoring benefits all stakeholders:

> For school administrators, mentoring aids recruitment and retention; for higher education institutions, it helps to ensure a smooth transition from campus to classroom; for teacher associations, it represents a new way to serve members and guarantee instructional quality; for teachers, it can represent the difference between success and failure; and for parents and students, it means better teaching.

When people consider investing time and energy in supporting a mentoring program, somewhere in their decision-making process—consciously or not—they will ask themselves, "What will my organization or I get out of this?" Now, don't get me wrong. The needs requiring satisfaction are not necessarily tangible or self-serving ones; more to the point, they are those categorized by Abraham H. Maslow in his seminal work, *Motivation and Personality* (1954). Maslow lists seven categories of needs that affect human behavior, five of which are relevant to our discussion:

- Social needs (affiliation, belonging, feeling part of something)
- Esteem needs (recognition, respect, feeling of worth)
- Need for self-actualization (putting abilities to work, using talents)

- Need to know and understand (intellectual curiosity, thirst for knowledge)
- Asthetic needs (order and balance, satisfying relationships)

According to Maslow, our behaviors and decisions are often determined by our desire to satisfy our strongest needs. A mentoring program may be able to address a participant's strongest needs in a variety of ways. For example, if you are a representative of the teacher's bargaining unit, you may see participation as a way to find out more about mentoring (the need to know and understand) so as to better represent your organization (the need for self-actualization) and to gain recognition and respect from peers (esteem needs). If you are a central office administrator, you may view participation as an opportunity to work more closely with like-minded colleagues (social need), provide meaningful professional development opportunities to staff (the need for self-actualization), and advocate for order and accountability (asthetic needs).

Of course, regardless of what group we represent, many of us support the concept of mentoring because, professionally, it is the right thing to do. We want to share and pass on our love of teaching and learning: That is our reward.

Exercise 1.2 Identify Potentially Committed People

Although a mentoring program must be tailor-made for your specific school or district, you should not ignore the lessons learned from other programs. For example, the NFIE (1999) points out in *Creating a Teacher Mentoring Program* that successful mentoring programs "are not run by those who prefer to work alone, either as individuals or organizations; [they] require partners."

The chart below lists the organizations or groups you should consider including as partners in building and maintaining an exemplary mentoring program. In the space next to each category, write in the name of the specific person(s) (include yourself) in your school or district who is a leader (designated or not) of that group, and who is likely to have a genuine interest in supporting a local mentoring program.

Organization or Group	*Representative(s) With Commitment Potential*
Teachers' bargaining unit	
Building administrators	
Central office administrators	
Designated mentor-teachers	
Nonmentoring veteran teachers	
First- or second-year teachers	
Noncertified staff	
Board of education	
PTO/PTA	
College/university faculty	
Retired teachers	
Business partnership	
Service clubs	
Local government	
Others:	

It is the commitment of these people—as well as their active participation—that will make your mentoring program exemplary.

Build and Reinforce Commitment

As we discussed earlier, people will be more likely to commit to the support of a mentoring program when they perceive that doing so resonates with their beliefs, that the program will probably be successful, and that by actively supporting the program, they will meet one or more of their basic needs. In the previous exercise, you identified potentially committed people who represent various groups of stakeholders in your school or district's mentoring program. In the following exercise, you will have the opportunity to refine your list in terms of how to reinforce each individual's potential commitment to support the program.

Exercise 1.3 Help Others to Commit

In the chart below, enter the names of the people you identified in Exercise 1.2. In the space provided, enter your best estimate of the mentoring-related beliefs, experiences, and kind of rewards that apply to each person. Of course, you can make only an educated guess about another person's beliefs and needs, but by doing this exercise, you will gain some insights as to what you might say or what resources you might provide to a person in order to enhance her or his commitment.

For example,

Organization	Person	Belief	Experience	Reward
Nonmentoring veteran teacher	Fran Smith	New teachers have a lot to learn	Member of professional development committee	Helps others grow (self-actualization)
Teachers' bargaining unit	Yolanda DiNapoli	New teachers need union support	On several school committees	Gains others' respect for union (esteem needs)

Now, it's your turn.

(continued)

Exercise 1.3 Help Others to Commit (continued)

Organization	Person	Belief	Experience	Reward
Teachers' bargaining unit				
Building administrators				
Central office administrators				
Designated mentor-teachers				
Nonmentoring veteran teachers				
First- or second-year teachers				
Noncertified staff				
Board of education				
PTO/PTA				
College/university faculty				
Retired teachers				
Business partnership				
Service clubs				
Local government				
Others:				

So, what do you think? Are you committed to enhancing your existing mentoring program or, if you do not yet have one, to developing an exemplary new program? Hopefully, you are, and if you did your homework, you have already identified others to join you. The next step is to invite them to do so. You probably will need to contact the various organizations and ask that they recommend or designate a representative, in which case it might be a good idea to urge the individuals you identified to actively seek that recommendation or designation.

Commitment is further developed through participation. In the following chapter, we set the stage for participation by examining the composition and *modus operandi* of a mentoring program committee.

Note

1. Adams, S. (2000, January 28) *Dilbert*. United Feature Syndicate, Inc.: Author.

2

Putting Commitment to Work

In the preceding chapter you identified a number of people in your school or district who have some degree of commitment to mentoring. Now consider this scenario: Some of these committed people are thinking that they would be willing to help—even participate in some sort of planning or implementation effort—if only somebody would ask them, but no one has.

Or imagine this scenario: Instead of waiting to be asked, the committed people are excitedly running around—individually or in groups—recruiting mentors, assigning them to work with new teachers, providing them with resources, arranging for their training, trying to rearrange schedules, writing memos, and. . . . *Whoa!*—slow down (unless you enjoy watching the "Law of Unanticipated Consequences" at work). Who are they recruiting as mentors? How, where, and why? To what criteria are they referring when matching mentors up with new teachers? What resources are they providing, and how will those resources be paid for? Most important, how and why are these decisions being made, and what are their effects on each other and on the district's educational system in general?

Either of the above scenarios—or another somewhere in between—is likely to be the one taking place in a school or district that has not yet effectively organized and focused the energy of people and organizations committed to the development, implementation, and maintenance of an exemplary mentoring program. It has not yet put together a committee of the committed.

"What, you want me to form another committee?" Well, yes, if your school or district has no program and is considering starting one—or even if there is a program, but no viable representative group is charged with providing a structure in which to plan, set policy, solve problems, make decisions, provide resources, assess, advocate for, and otherwise guide and support mentoring.

A word of caution here: It may be tempting for one person—usually an assistant superintendent or a professional development coordinator—

unilaterally to plan and implement a mentoring program, but experience has shown over and over again that representation from as many areas of the education community as possible should be included in the process if it is to continue to develop over time. If, for example, the building principal is not directly involved or if the teacher's association is kept out of the process, there is little chance that mentoring will ever become part of the institutional fabric.

Even if your school or district already has a mentoring committee or planning team in place to provide leadership, structure, and oversight to an existing mentoring program, the discussions and exercises in this chapter will help fine-tune the way that group operates.

However, before we get into the specifics of committees and their functions, let's consider the foundation upon which a mentoring program must rest. I refer, of course, to the willingness of people—especially those with the power to back up their determination with action—to affirm publicly their belief in and readiness to support the development and maintenance of an exemplary mentoring program.

Public Affirmation

One of the most consistent themes associated with exemplary mentoring programs is a clear message of commitment from the local board of education saying, in effect, "We value the teachers new to our district, and consider mentoring by their experienced colleagues to be fundamental to their professional growth." If the school board has not yet voiced such a commitment, a proposal should be made to the board calling upon it to establish the mentoring of new teachers as district policy.

Following is an example of a new teacher mentoring policy proposal for adoption by a board of education. Although you are free to copy it verbatim, please consider not doing so, because each district should tailor such a document to its own needs, situation, and culture.

A Policy Statement on Mentoring New Teachers Proposed for Adoption by the _____ Board of Education

Rationale: The cornerstone of quality education is what happens between the educator and the student. Therefore, we expect our teachers to have and to continue to develop the skills, knowledge, and understanding needed in order for their interactions with students to be highly effective.

During the next 10 years, we expect to hire a larger number of new teachers than we have in the past decade. The increased need for new teachers is the result of anticipated teacher retirements, increased student enrollments, and plans for smaller class size.

These new teachers will bring with them a strong knowledge base and an eagerness to teach. Research and experience suggest, however, that without the advantage of a program that provides for and supports the mentoring of beginning teachers by their experienced colleagues, over 30% of new teachers will leave the profession after their first year or two, and others who do remain will probably take longer than otherwise to reach their full professional potential.

Because we value highly the teachers new to our school/district, and consider mentoring by their experienced colleagues to be fundamental to their professional growth and, therefore, to their ability to better serve our children, it is essential that the district develop and maintain an effective mentoring program for new teachers. Therefore,

Policy: The _____ Board of Education will
    1. Provide for a planned, ongoing mentoring program for new teachers including funds and time for planning and implementation
    2. Direct the Superintendent to establish a planning and implementation committee composed of representatives from the Board of Education, administration, and teachers' local professional association, and other appropriate persons. The committee shall be responsible to the Superintendent for planning, developing, implementing, managing, and evaluating an induction and mentoring program for new teachers.
    3. Direct the Superintendent to report semiannually to the Board of Education on the mentoring program and its effect, with recommendations for changes as needed.

Whether such a proposal is made before or after a planning committee is formed will depend on the proposers' wisdom and sense of timing and on the procedure preferred by the board. In either event, whoever makes the proposal should first have gathered relevant data about their own district, have reviewed current literature and practices on mentoring and mentoring programs, and be prepared to articulate the philosophy, mission, and goals of their proposed program.

The proposers should also have their act together in terms of their presentation to the board; that is, they should know when to present, what the desired outcomes of the presentation are, the presentation's content and design, what materials and equipment will be needed, and who will prepare, deliver, and follow up on the presentation. The presentation will be greatly enhanced by written evidence that the proposal was developed and is supported by the local teachers' organization, building and central office staff and administrators, parent groups, school councils, the teacher center, business partners, and college or university faculty. It has been pointed out that without the support of those who affect or are affected by the program, it may fall short of its intended outcomes or even fail. It is also necessary to note that although the development of the program may be a collaborative process, there frequently is a champion among the collaborators—someone who has a vision for the program, persuades others to adopt or adapt that vision, and enables the group to achieve it (Newton et al., 1994).

The Planning and Implementation Committee: Its Modus Operandi

The mentoring program committee is a decision-making group. How it makes decisions and how it solves problems will largely determine the quantity and quality of its decisions. We will examine problem solving and decision making shortly; but first, and perhaps even more basic to the effective functioning of the group, is the way individual members interact.

Committee Dynamics

Let's eavesdrop on the Xville School District's Monday afternoon Mentoring Planning Committee meeting, which is about to begin. Chuck, a middle school assistant principal and elected chair of the group, claps his hands together and says

"Okay, people, let's get started." He points to the agenda on the chalkboard. "Lots to get through today."

At one end of the table, Ben and Alice are quietly holding a side conversation, which continues on even when Chuck introduces the first item on the agenda: the need for additional mentors.

"We anticipate hiring new art, music, and physical education teachers next year and have no trained mentors available in those categories or money to train any new ones. Any suggestions? Ben? Alice?"

"Huh?" Ben mumbles.

Anne, a kindergarten teacher, raises her hand. "Is it really necessary that a mentor be someone from the same discipline? I mean. . . ."

Darlene interrupts Anne. "We've been over this before. I want my new math teachers to be mentored only by experienced math teachers—no matter what grade they teach. Let's move on."

Ethel, the assistant superintendent, stands up, peers around the table, nods and smiles almost imperceptibly toward Darlene, then turns to Anne and gives her *the look*. Anne pushes away from the table and glances at the floor. Everyone else stops what they are doing and looks at Ethel. "I propose we just go ahead and assign our older art, music, and phys. ed. teachers to the new teachers in their respective areas."

Ben whispers to Alice, "I don't recall any of the music teachers or the other 'specials' ever being trained as mentors."

"Shhh," says Alice.

When Ethel finishes her proposal, Chuck calls for discussion. No one says anything. Fred, the high school guidance counselor, puts his hand on Chuck's shoulder and whispers something into his ear. Chuck nods and clears his throat. "Anne, you had some concerns about this issue. Is there anything you want to say?"

Silence, then, "No, I . . . umm, well, yes, I do. I think . . ."

We have heard enough for now, so let's quietly leave. Typical or not, the Xville scenario illustrates some of the dynamics that may be in play while your school's or district's committee is meeting. The following exercise will help you become aware of these dynamics, point out some ways to reduce behaviors that stifle participation, and suggest strategies to reinforce behaviors that promote active participation.

Exercise 2.1   What's Going On in Your Committee?

A committee functions best when there are productive interpersonal relationships among committee members. Let's gather some data. Think back to your last committee meeting or note what goes on during your next one. In the charts below, write in the name(s) of the appropriate individual(s) or the information that an item calls for. Don't forget to include yourself.

Verbal Participation

Who talks often?	
Who seldom talks?	
Who usually talks to whom?	
When do these patterns change?	

Influence

When they talk, others listen and act.	
When they talk, others ignore or change the subject.	
Talk or not, who are the real leaders/movers?	
Is there a struggle for leadership? Between whom?	

Dysfunctional Behavior

Who interrupts?	
Who holds side conversations?	
Who changes the topic prematurely?	
Who "puts down" other members?	
Who withdraws from the discussion?	

Exercise 2.1 (continued)

Facilitating Roles

Who begins discussions?	
Who seeks information and opinions?	
Who gives information and opinions?	

Facilitating Roles

Who clarifies?	
Who summarizes?	
Who sets standards?	
Who reduces tension?	
Who encourages others to participate?	

Now that you have a sense of the group's dynamics—how various individuals interact with others in various situations—what can you do to facilitate productive interpersonal relationships among committee members? Here are some suggestions:

- *Reinforce positive behavior.* Feed back your appreciation. Let folks know that you noticed what they did or said and how it was helpful.

- *Encourage others to participate in discussions.* Ask individuals by name for their opinion and recognize their contributions.

- *Respect everyone's contribution.* See to it that when someone presents an idea or thought to the discussion, it is acknowledged and, if appropriate, responded to.

- *Be an assertive, contributing, and sensitive member.* Prepare your thoughts as well as possible in advance, and present them fully and logically; listen to others and be ready to modify your own opinion on the basis of logic and understanding; avoid changing your mind only to avoid conflict; and view differences of opinion as helpful to decision making. The best decision making happens when people feel safe.

Group Decision Making

Members of the school's or district's mentoring committee will need to make many group decisions, and they will be expected to support those decisions. It is not always easy for a group to arrive at a decision upon which every member will agree. Individuals tend to favor solutions they propose. Sometimes an individual, for various reasons, may decide not to favor one solution over another, but simply to go along with the majority or with a trusted colleague. Individuals are inclined to help implement and otherwise support decisions that they have helped to make. Therefore, a productive committee is dependent on full participation by all its members in its decision-making process.

Here are the most common group decision-making methods:

- An individual agrees—or a subcommittee is formed—to investigate an issue, report findings to the full committee, and to make recommendations. On the one hand, this procedure allows several issues to be researched simultaneously while cutting down on the amount of time required from each person. On the other hand, there may be a tendency for the individual or subgroup to have formed such a strong opinion that they emphasize data that agree with their viewpoint and attempt to cut short any dissenting discussion.

The investigated issue is then put through one of the following processes.

- The question is put to a *majority vote*. Usually following *Robert's Rules of Order*, a motion is made and seconded, a vote is taken, and more than half of the members (if there is a quorum present) agree or disagree. This procedure can save time, but if the proposal passes, those who voted against it may not fully support the decision.

- The *unanimous vote* is similar to the majority vote, except that all voting members must agree in order for the proposal to pass. Of course, one person can block a decision by disagreeing. There is also the possibility that someone may feel obligated to agree, but again, not really support the decision.

- Like the two methods above, *consensus* is a process in which all parties actively discuss the issues around the decision to be made. The difference, however, is that the ideas and feelings of all members are integrated into a group decision that, in order to be accepted, must have the agreement of each member to support it. During the consensus process, discussions and straw polls take place, modifications of the original proposal are considered, attempts are made to find common points of agreement, and, finally, all involved make a genuine commitment to implementation.

As you might imagine, decision by consensus is usually difficult to attain and will consume more time than other methods. However, as the energies of the group become more focused on the problem at hand (rather than on defending individual points of view), the quality of the decision tends to be enhanced. Furthermore, the decision itself is likely to be more vigorously implemented than if made by other methods, such as the use of majority power (voting), minority power (persuasion), or compromise.

Realistically, of course, not every decision made by consensus will meet everyone's unqualified approval. There should, however, be a general indication of support from all members before consensus is considered to have taken place. Because decision by consensus usually takes a great deal more time than other methods, the process may prove frustrating to some. If, however, each group member takes the time needed to listen for understanding, to consider all other members' views, and to make her or his own views known, then ultimately the committee will make high-quality decisions that will be well supported.

Beware the Illusion of Agreement

On April 17, 1961, a brigade of about 1,400 Cuban exiles, aided by the U.S. Navy, Air Force, and CIA, invaded the swampy coast of Cuba at the Bay of Pigs. The rest, as the saying goes, is history. Nothing went as planned, and by the third day the approximately 1,200 invaders who had not been killed by Castro's 20,000 well-equipped troops, were captured and ignominiously led off to prison camps.

The irony of the Bay of Pigs fiasco—and the reason I refer to it here—is that the decision to go ahead with the ill-conceived plan was made by consensus of a popular president and a group of advisors who, as author Irving L. Janis (1972) describes them, had "considerable intellectual talent, [were] capable of objective, rational analysis, and [were] accustomed to speaking their minds."

According to Janis, "When a group of people who respect each other's opinions arrive at a unanimous view, each member is likely to feel that the belief must be true. This reliance on consensual validation tends to replace individual critical thinking and reality testing, unless there are clear-cut disagreements among the members." Janis suggests that had even one senior advisor opposed the adventure during the group's meetings, President Kennedy would have canceled it. No one spoke against it publicly, although privately—it was reported later—several voiced their doubts.

Ironically, the more amiable and cohesive your committee, the greater the danger that independent critical thinking will be replaced by what Janis calls *groupthink*. A built-in adversary—a designated "devil's advocate"—can help dispel groupthink. The concept of groupthink need not cause you any paranoia, but by being aware of its possibility, your committee's decision making will be less susceptible to miscalculation.

In summary, if your mentoring program . . .

- Is publicly affirmed by board of education members who commit themselves in writing to the belief that mentoring is a powerful way to retain and develop new teachers

- Is planned and implemented by committee members who represent organizations and groups that are committed to the belief that mentoring is a powerful way to develop and retain new teachers

- Is overseen by a committee whose *modus operandi* is collaborative decision making and whose members are sensitive to the group dynamics within which the committee operates

. . . then chances are your district has put the commitment of its people to work in such a way as to ensure a firm foundation for the development and ongoing support of an exemplary mentoring program.

3

The Macrosystem

Sometimes we fail to see the forest for the trees. Your mentoring program is part of a larger system, and, like a young sapling in a mature grove, it is affected by and in turn affects its surroundings. This chapter looks at the jungle of government, professional, higher education, and local mandates, guidelines, policies, and practices, and considers how they influence the shape and the structure of individual elements in a mentoring program. When we understand the nature of the wilderness encircling our local programs, we can avoid the pitfalls and direct the nurturing qualities inherent in that labyrinth. By ignoring the macrosystem's potential to support, we run the risk of allowing it to stifle.

State Mandates, Guidelines, and Incentives

When I was a consultant with the Connecticut State Department of Education, I had the marvelous opportunity to talk informally about teaching and learning with many educational leaders, several of whom were responsible for developing and directing mentoring programs for their local districts. I would like to share with you a small portion of one of these conversations, because it relates directly to how state initiatives can be perceived, and how that perception can influence local action.

Paul (not his real name) was Chair of the Professional Development Committee in one of the state's larger cities. He told me one day how frustrating it was to try to get the school board to agree to a proposal his committee had made. The proposal was based on solid research, and addressed one of the good practices in professional development that had been identified by the National Staff Development Council.

"Paul," I reminded him, "what you propose is also recognized as good practice, and is highly recommended by the State Department of Education in its published guidelines. Is your board familiar with those guidelines?"

"Yes, but evidently the guidelines don't seem to be taken very seriously."

"Is there any way the Department of Education could support your proposal?"

"Sure. Make it mandatory and fund it!"

State legislatures and boards of education in the majority of states must have heard Paul, or others like him, because they decided to mandate—and in many cases fund—the mentoring of new teachers. However, as Carmen Giebelhaus from the Ohio Department of Education observed during a symposium presented at the October 15, 1998, meeting of the Mid-Western Educational Research Association in Chicago, even when mentoring is required,

> States send a clear message regarding [its] importance by the amount of funds that are allocated. Some states have initiated the "unfunded mandate," which guarantees uneven compliance or in many cases non-compliance! . . . If a mentoring and support system for beginning teachers is mandated, then the funding should accompany the law.

As an aside, a state may hesitate to require a procedure because it then feels obliged to fund what it mandates; instead, it opts to exert influence by presenting that action as a guideline or standard.

Consistent with systems theory, the macrosystem of state mandates and funding (or lack thereof) will affect your local mentoring committee's decisions. In addition, when state mandates and funding change, local change will follow. Therefore, your local committee must be clear about what is actually mandated and thus *must* be followed, and what is a guideline or recommendation and need only be seriously considered. The distinction between mandates and guidelines or standards is important because, as guidelines or standards may not legally be required, you can decide not to follow one if it is not appropriate to your local situation. For example, a standard that calls for a mentor to be licensed and teaching in the same discipline as the beginning teacher, even though desirable and worth striving for, may not always be possible in a small district. Be aware, however, that sometimes state funding is dependent on compliance with guidelines.

Another important consideration about state education mandates is that in most cases the legislation and its related regulations specify *what* is to be done, but not necessarily *how.* There is often more latitude in local decision making and implementation than may initially meet the eye. In other words, the onus as well as the responsibility for the quality of the local program lies with the local planners and implementers. Of course, your committee should also be up to date as to what entitlements and other funding opportunities (e.g., competitive grants, stipends, or bonuses) are available and how they can be accessed.

Many states that currently have regulations requiring mentoring for new teachers are revising those mandates with an eye toward strengthening their impact. For example, some recently proposed revisions (effective September 2001) in the *Regulations for the Certification of Educational Personnel in Massachusetts* highlight the increasingly important role mentoring programs for new teachers are expected to have in the Commonwealth's public schools. Massachusetts public school districts have been required for a couple of years to provide an induction program for beginning teachers. A recent revision established a set of standards that would be used to judge the quality of these programs.

Let's assume that I am a member of the mentoring program committee in a small district in Massachusetts and have a copy of the proposed new standards. After examining them, I underline the words in each standard that seem to have implications for our local program, and note the kinds of impact those revisions might have. For example, here is how I might analyze two of the Massachusetts standards.

Standard: *All* beginning teachers are assigned to a *trained* mentor.

Implication: Our little district will have four new teachers next year: preschool, high school calculus, elementary special education, and a districtwide instrumental music teacher. We have a policy that mentors must come from the same discipline and/or grade level as their mentees. Our only experienced music teacher is willing to mentor the new person, but refuses to be trained as a mentor.

Standard: Beginning in 2005, *only master teachers* will be eligible to serve as *formal* mentors of preservice or beginning teachers. [Note: The regulations specify criteria for designation as a master teacher.]

Implication: Our projections are that there will not be enough master teachers to go around. Do we assign some master teachers more than one new teacher? If so, how will we provide extra time and/or money? Can we legally use non–master teachers as *informal* mentors? If so, should they be trained and compensated?

Exercise 3.1 Who Is Your State Department of Education Contact? What Does Your State Require? Recommend? Fund?

If you don't already know, find out the name, phone number, mailing address, and e-mail address of your state's Department of Education (DOE) person responsible for new teacher induction and mentoring. Find it on your state's Internet web page or call the department's "information" phone number. When you contact the appropriate DOE person, introduce yourself. Ask for a copy of your state's current legislation, regulations, guidelines, funding opportunities, and other mentoring-related materials along with any proposed revisions. In most, if not all cases, mentoring requirements are linked to performance-based licensing regulations for new teachers. Share the information and material with your local committee members. Note whether there are any recent or proposed changes that might require changes in your current program.

Higher Education

Without question, academia is where most of the research and analysis that has spurred and informed the development of beginning teacher induction and mentoring programs has taken place—and it probably will continue to do so. There are other important ways in which your program can benefit from college or university departments or schools of education; faculty exchanges, professional development schools, cooperative action research, in-house professional development seminars, teacher preparation, and mentor training are examples. Let's look at two of these areas—teacher preparation and mentor training—in terms of their potential for interaction with your mentoring program.

In the teacher preparation process, the climax occurs in the student-teaching or practicum experience, where universities collaborate with schools to create clinical learning environments for aspiring teachers. This is the time—usually during an extended fifth year or graduate program—in which practice teaching is supervised by college faculty and guided by a school cooperative teacher or mentor. Should your mentoring program enter into such an arrangement with an institution of higher education? There are several advantages. Such a relationship can be seen as a professional development opportunity for both the student teacher and the cooperating teacher/mentor. It also is common practice for a cooperating teacher/mentor to receive a stipend and/or other compensation from the college, such as a tuition voucher or appointment as adjunct faculty.

Some schools and districts have found it advantageous to use university professors as mentors to some of their first-year teachers. The Celina (Ohio) City School District, for example, has such a contractual arrangement with the Wright State University (WSU) education faculty. The

Celina-WSU relationship is based on three assumptions: that (a) university education professors are able to address novice teachers' instructional needs; (b) education professors will be more accessible than public school administrators and teachers; and (c) professors can address first-year teacher problems collaboratively with both the beginning teacher and school administrators, and still maintain confidentiality.

Mentor training is sometimes provided by higher-education professors directly or in conjunction with training programs sponsored by their college or university. Training is sometimes arranged exclusively for mentors in one or two schools or districts; at other times, it is scheduled at the college itself with registration open to teachers from all area school districts.

Exercise 3.2 How Colleges and Universities Can Help Your Program

Many school districts have arrangements with a neighboring college or university in areas other than mentoring, for example in student teaching, lab school, on-site campus, or a visiting professor program. This exercise asks you to (a) take inventory of ways in which your school or district currently interacts with higher education, (b) brainstorm how these interactions might affect or support the mentoring system, and (c) look at the various components of your mentoring program and consider how they might be strengthened by interacting with schools of education.

In the columns below, list any cooperative arrangement your school or district already has in place and how that arrangement might be extended to benefit the mentoring program.

For example, if you rely on nearby college faculty to provide leadership for professional development workshops, perhaps they can extend that service by training mentors to be trainers.

Another example would be if you were looking for ways to recognize or compensate mentors, perhaps a college would consider inviting mentors as guest presenters in teacher preparation or graduate leadership classes (a stipend would be appreciated).

Existing College-School Interaction	Potential for Mentoring Program

Exercise 3.2 (continued)

Now look at the potential for school-college interaction from another perspective. Reverse the process: List your major mentoring program components in the first column below, and consider how a local college or university might play a productive role in that area.

Mentoring Component	Potential Role for College

Professional Associations and Organizations

The AFT, NEA, NASSP, NAESP, American Association of School Administrators (AASA), ASCD, NSDC, Phi Delta Kappa (PDK), International Mentoring Association (IMA, which is housed at Western Michigan University in Kalamazoo), American Association of Colleges for Teacher Education (AACTE), and American Educational Research Association (AERA) are some of the prestigious educational organizations that have been at the forefront of advocacy for mentoring over the past decade or two. Most have crafted resolutions supporting new teacher induction, sponsored and conducted conferences on mentoring issues, devoted issues of their journals to mentoring, and published mentoring guidelines and training materials.

ASCD, for example, has an active mentoring committee, has produced mentor training materials, and has devoted the May 1999 issue of its widely read publication, *Education Leadership*, to mentoring.

AERA has a mentoring special interest group (SIG) that shares information and research and meets during the organization's annual meetings.

NASSP has identified four chronological phases in the effective induction process for new teachers. The association has also produced a set of comprehensive materials for the development of instructional leaders that have been adapted by the South Carolina Department of Education for use in training mentor teachers in the state.

These organizations and others like them are highly respected and have enormous influence. Their policies and materials are distributed to large constituencies, and can help form the practical and philosophical underpinnings for local programs such as yours. Wherever possible, the planning, implementation, and evaluation of mentoring programs must be negotiated or cooperatively developed *from the beginning* by the school district and the local affiliate. Relevant literature, as well as my own experience with districts that have developed a program unilaterally, has shown that unless teacher associations are included from the "get-go" as partners, chances are that the endeavor will constantly be plagued with problems.

Exercise 3.3 Reinforce Professional Support

Acquire professional education association and organization policies, recommendations, and materials that favor and support mentoring. If and when appropriate, and in the spirit of a reminder, share them with local members of those organizations.

The Internal Macrosystem

Just as the profusion of trees in a vast forest can overwhelm an individual tree, so, too, can the plethora of programs in an established school system influence the growth of a new program. Within every school and district there is a set of systems—mentoring is probably one of the newer ones in the set—that at first blush seem unrelated, yet actually affect the others more often than realized. Let's look briefly at the potential effect some of these sister systems have on a local mentoring program, and what impact a change in one can engender in another.

Included in the system of systems that make up the typical district's internal macrosystem are retirement policies and patterns, curriculum revision, class size and schedules, teacher supervision and evaluation, student demographics, administrative and board policy development, budgets and budgeting, professional development, school remodeling and construction, and parent organizations.

Relationships between these systems and the mentoring program are rather straightforward and generally have to do with stipends, substitutes, training, materials, consultants, travel, focus of mentor-mentee interactions, confidentially, documentation, time, location, accountability, compensation, working conditions, and roles. The committee will need to consider these ubiquitous areas when developing the mentoring program, and will need to be cognizant of any changes in them that might affect their program. The following exercise will help you anticipate how to benefit from such change.

Exercise 3.4 *Take Advantage of Change*

Imagine this scenario: Your school district has been under a lot of pressure to do something special for its gifted and talented students. The school board directs the superintendent to institute a summer school program for these students. The board will fund the development of a program that is innovative and creative—*not* remedial. They want no grades or report cards, and special curricula should be developed that will attract and challenge the district's brightest kids.

In the space provided, briefly respond to the three questions below as they relate to the above scenario.

1. How might the mentoring program benefit from this opportunity?

_____

_____

_____

_____

_____

2. How might the mentoring program help the summer school?

_____

_____

_____

_____

_____

3. What changes in the mentoring program might be needed as a result of what you propose in response to questions 1 and 2?

_____

_____

_____

_____

_____

_____

Here, briefly, is how one district's mentoring program responded to the scenario in Exercise 3.4:

1. Mentors and mentees developed the curriculum together. The fact that they were recognized as peers gave the mentees a great deal of confidence and helped solidify the mentor-mentee relationship. The many discussions and research opportunities provided a powerful learning experience for both mentors and mentees. Many of the first-year teachers taught in the summer program, thereby gaining additional experience.

2. The cutting edge theories gleaned from recent college courses, combined with the fresh way of thinking and the exuberance typical of first-year teachers, led to a more creative and youth-oriented program than might otherwise have been the case. In addition, all of the participating new teachers reported having been energized by the experience and all have remained in the profession.

3. To help mentors and mentees meet the need to develop a creative and innovative curriculum, the program provided them with training in curriculum design and use of the Internet for research. Additional training for mentors focused on peer-mentoring issues. The previous mentoring schedule was adjusted to accommodate the project, and the program's budget was increased to accommodate the additional training.

The Power of Culture and Tradition

There are other internal systems—unofficial and subtle—working within virtually all schools and districts that could have as much to say about the mentoring program as do the formal ones. I am referring to culture (as in, "This is the way we do things around here") and tradition (as in, "This is the way we've always done them"). The following illustrates how ignoring the power of culture and tradition almost undermined a school district's otherwise well-planned mentoring program.

This was the first year of the Eastbank (fictitious name, real scenario) School District's new mentoring program. The planning committee—a dedicated group of committed teachers and administrators—had worked for two years to develop what they and the local college's school of education faculty members who had worked with them considered to be an excellent program design—and it was. It had all the elements an exemplary program should have.

About midway through the first year of the program, during one of their monthly "touching bases" meetings, the middle and high school mentors discovered that many of their mentees were having a common set of problems: constantly having to deal with unruly students, no time to get their rooms ready for the next class, lots of stress, and physical exhaustion. These issues took so much of the time mentors spent meeting with their mentees that they seldom got to curriculum and instruction issues. All this was frustrating to the mentors, as well as rather surprising. After all, the new group of teachers was bright and well prepared: They should be ready for help with teaching by now, not still stuck on noninstructional issues.

"You know," offered Brian, a high school history teacher and mentor, "I recall my first year teaching. I had the same experience as my mentee. I hung in there because I wanted desperately to teach, but a couple of other beginners resigned after the first year."

Nadine, a middle school English teacher and mentor nodded in agreement. "I had the same experience during my first year," she said. "The situation eased during the next few years. I remember that as a new teacher I was assigned the lowest section classes, the most difficult students, the worst schedules, and the most demanding extra duties. Is this still the case?"

"It sure is," answered Fran, a mentor with 34 years teaching experience. "In fact, our contract supports this by allowing senior teachers to pick which class they want to teach in which school."

At their next meeting, Fran reported that she had discussed with other veteran teachers the practice of assigning new teachers the most difficult students and schedules. She was shocked—but not surprised—by comments from some of her nonmentoring colleagues:

"These new kids on the block ought to be in the toughest classrooms. They are young, they are strong, and they have the latest pedagogical skills."

"We've always done it this way. We've all paid our dues. We've got seniority now and deserve the consideration we receive."

Brian slapped his palm on the table. "Wow! That last statement reminds me of the rationale behind the practice of hazing in my old college fraternity."

"Hazing was a tradition in my sorority, too," added Nadine.

"I think we've got things backward, here," Fran chimed in. "A new teacher should have a lighter load than an experienced teacher; after all, a new teacher needs time to adjust to the difference between theory and practice and time to prepare for classes."

"Absolutely!" added Brian. "When my mentee meets with me, he needs to be less stressed out and more focused than he usually is. I don't believe I'm compromising confidentiality here when I tell you that my mentee said he would have quit by now if he hadn't had a mentor."

The Eastbank mentoring committee has tried to change the situation, but so far with no success. However, now that the mentors understand the effects of the "tradition," they are better able to work within it.

The Spector of Past Experience

A variation of culture and tradition is the specter of past experience. A glaring example of how past experience almost negated the efforts of a district to develop a new teacher mentoring program took place in the suburban New England town of South Riverton (not the town's real name).

Five years ago, the South Riverton superintendent and his administrator's council, unable to find as much time as they would like to devote to teacher supervision and evaluation, unilaterally implemented the "South Riverton Peer-Mentoring Program," in which a teacher would observe a colleague in the classroom and submit a written report to the principal for follow-up. Within six months, the word *mentoring* had become anathema in South Riverton. No teacher would have anything to do with mentoring—the term smacked of teachers spying on one another, unfair practices, breech of contract, and overall unprofessionalism. The teacher's association charged that peer mentoring had become just another word for teacher evaluation. Unofficially, but effectively, teachers boycotted the program by not scheduling or keeping peer-mentoring appointments, checking "excellent" on every item of the report, and by contesting the matching of specific mentors to other specific teachers. For all practical purposes, the program ceased to function.

When a new superintendent came to South Riverton a couple of years ago, she found that over 20% of the district's teachers would be retiring over the next three years, and that a growing population would soon require additional teachers. Consequently, she directed that a planning committee be formed to set up a mentoring program for new teachers. She met with board members, groups of educators, and townspeople—both separately and together—who, after much discussion, agreed that new teachers must have the opportunity to interact with experienced teachers throughout at least their first year of teaching. The teacher's association, although agreeing with the idea in principle, cited the fiasco of five years earlier and refused to support anything called a "mentoring program." After a great deal of discussion and negotiation, the board eventually adopted a policy, reflected in a negotiated revision of the teacher's contract, that teachers are to be evaluated by staff trained and credentialed for that purpose, not by peers. The debilitating memory of past experience, however, continued to echo throughout various attempts to develop a new teacher induction program. Finely, consensus was reached on a name for their new endeavor: Beginning Teacher Induction and Support (note the conspicuous absence of the word *mentoring*). The program is now under way—developed and run by a committee that includes committed union representation.

In summary, mentoring is one of many programs in an internal macrosystem, each of which interacts with the others to make up a local school or district. Because these programs interact, they are dependent on one another; because each program is part of a larger macrosystem, change in one impels change in the others. Consequently, a mentoring program committee needs (a) to be familiar with the other programs in their school or district (e.g., budget, curriculum, scheduling, or space allotment programs) and how those programs relate to the mentoring; (b) to be aware of any changes in those programs and how such changes might affect mentoring; and (c) to be proactive in influencing the direction of change in other components so as to best support the mentoring effort. These same considerations also hold true for a mentoring program's relationship with government, professional, and higher-education macrosystems. In the following chapters, we will keep these macrosystems in mind, and consider how they might apply to the topic at hand.

4

Roles and Responsibilities

(It Takes a Community to Induct a Teacher)

One of these days, when the situation presents itself, I'll ask a gathering of educators—the larger and more diversified, the better—this question: "Who here is responsible for the induction into the profession of your school's or district's new teachers?" I would like to think that most would raise their hands, having accepted induction as part of their professional obligation, but I'd give 10 to 1 odds that the number would be 10% to 20%. "No! No!" I'd cry . . . but silently, inside myself. Outwardly, I'd keep my composure, and hope that eventually everyone would realize for himself or herself that as educators we all have that responsibility. Nurturing and developing a new teacher is a collaborative effort.

There is power in such collaboration. When the process of mentoring new teachers has been collaborative, those involved are likely to share in the program's vision and goals. When collaboration has not occurred, consensus alone is not enough to allow them to move ahead. "Together we know more than any one of us knows individually. Thus . . . we have an obligation to share knowledge, wisdom, and council with our colleagues, and to seek such from them in return" (*Teacher—A New Definition and Model for Development and Evaluation,* 1992).

Mentors and mentoring committee members are only two of several groups of people in an education community that are responsible for raising a teacher. The National Foundation for the Improvement of Education (1999) suggests, for example, that

> a district-level instructional program, a school-based instructional team, or both might be available to provide protégés with training and assistance pertaining to academic content, curriculum development, and student assessments. An effective mentor collaborates in this process . . . but should not be held solely responsible for ensuring that protégés have a full understanding of a school's

instructional program. This obligation must be shared more broadly by the entire faculty and administration.

Harry and Rosemary Wong (2000) recognize the power of a team approach to new teacher induction when they cite the approach used in the El Reno (Oklahoma) Public School District. The El Reno induction program

> enlists the ongoing support of staff development members, principals, coordinators, mentor teachers, school board members, and supervisory staff members in order to ensure that their new teachers are highly trained and adequately supported. . . . [El Reno's] newly hired teachers, whether novice or veteran teachers, get a full week of orientation to the school district and training in classroom management and instructional strategies. Both administrators and teachers provide the week's training with some of the sessions conducted by the district's mentor teachers who continue to provide year-long support for the inductees.

Earlier, we examined roles and responsibilities of mentoring committee members. In this chapter, we will survey the roles and responsibilities of just about everyone else in the teaching and learning community when it comes to the development of new teachers.

Administrators

It is critical that school and district administrators understand the value of mentoring. Whether or not you are an administrator, it is important to remind yourself every now and then that it makes pragmatic sense to support the mentoring of new teachers. A new teacher's initial set of experiences is bound to have an impact on professional performance and student learning for the rest of his or her career.

The time spent inducting a new teacher into the working culture can determine how, when, or even if he or she will contribute to several critical issues associated with school improvement and reform. For example, effective mentoring will improve the probability that (a) a new teacher will remain in the profession long enough to justify the district's investment, (b) a new teacher's individual performance will continue to grow, and (c) the investment in a new teacher will pay off sooner and better in terms of student success and overall school climate.

Although it is important that all administrators take responsibility for the development of a new teacher, the role of the building principal is probably the most critical. During a symposium presented at the 1998 annual meeting of the Mid-Western Educational Research Association in Chicago, Barbara L. Brock of Creighton University postulated the following:

[the principal's role] is to coordinate the mentorship program to insure that the goals of the mentors are in tangent with other supervisors who work with the beginners. Unfortunately, some principals cease active participation in the mentorship process once the mentors have been assigned. They fail to realize that beginning teachers want and need interaction with and feedback from their principal.

Brock goes on to say that "beginning teachers need to know what the principal's expectations are for instructional methods, time management, discipline, grading, and student achievement. . . . [T]he principal is the person whom they need to please and who will likely evaluate them."

Brother Thomas Puccio, Principal of Malden (Massachusetts) Catholic High School, is an outstanding example of an administrator who values new teachers and their development. In January 1999, both *U.S. News and World Report* magazine and the ABC television network's *Good Morning America* recognized Malden Catholic High School's exemplary teacher-mentoring program and cited the role of Principal Puccio in its success. The following excerpts from a conversation I had with Brother Thomas illustrate his leadership role in his school's mentoring process.

Hal: I know that you meet with *all* your teachers individually on a regular basis, Tom. Do you arrange *additional* meetings with new teachers?

Tom: Yes, in addition to meeting with them as individuals as often as I can, I also schedule monthly meetings with all first- and second-year teachers. We gather as a group after school for about an hour. We discuss some topics that are current in the school calendar, but more particularly the meetings are to discuss assigned chapters from *The Skillful Teacher* [Saphier & Gower, 1997]. I invite mentors to join us at a couple of specific sessions during the year so we can share experiences.

Hal: I notice your mentoring program requires mentors and mentees to schedule reciprocal class visits on a regular basis. How do you schedule such visits?

Tom: I am not involved in scheduling those visits. I try to encourage and support it by some creative master scheduling. I've even been taken up on my occasional offers to cover classes for mentors and colleagues. I use an occasional memo to mentors or an article on the topic to serve as gentle reminders.

There are other roles and responsibilities administrators can take on. For example, they can

- Assign beginning teachers a moderate teaching load with relatively few preparations, few extracurricular duties, and a schedule compatible with the mentor's

- Express appreciation to school and district mentors, both privately and in public

- Respect the confidential relationship between mentors and mentees

- Help develop faculty and community support for the program

- Serve as members of the mentoring program planning and implementation committee

- Coordinate mentoring with other programs throughout the school or district

- Establish relationships with local colleges and universities that will benefit the mentoring program

Supervisors

Instructional supervisors, subject coordinators, and department chairs have many of the same roles and responsibilities as administrators in regard to the mentoring program. In addition to undertaking many of the same mentoring-related responsibilities as administrators, they can be excellent resources to both mentors and mentees for subject-specific assistance and for curriculum implementation and articulation.

Nonmentoring Veteran Teachers

There are probably veteran teachers in your school district who are not serving as mentors. Like their colleagues who are mentors, they possess a combination of solid professional experience and firsthand familiarity with local culture. If given the opportunity, these teachers can also play an important role in the development of their novice colleagues. Nonmentoring teachers can participate in planning groups, help select mentors, and take part in the evaluation of the mentoring program. Perhaps more important, they can provide direct assistance to new teachers, either in ways suggested by mentors or when requested directly by the novice.

For example, while observing his mentee teaching a seventh-grade science laboratory class, Keith noticed that students were having difficulty using microscopes. During the postobservation conference, Keith pointed this out to his mentee, Nan. Nan replied that she was aware of the situation, but did not know what to do about it, because she was unfamiliar with the focusing mechanism on the model of microscope in her classroom. Keith suggested that Nan discuss the situation with a 20-year veteran who taught another section of the class in a similarly equipped classroom down the hall. Keith offered to arrange for the two to meet. Nan thanked him, but said she would contact the teacher down the hall and follow through on her own. The veteran teacher was pleased to have been asked, and not only showed Nan how to use the microscopes, but also spent many hours during the rest of the year sharing lesson plans and instructional strategies.

A more formal way veteran teachers can share their knowledge and experience is by making themselves available as presenters of specific topics during first-year teacher meetings, or as on-call consultants to individual new teachers. The professional development committee of XYZ High School (not its real name) began such a program a few years ago: They call it Sharing Our Skills (S.O.S.). Although S.O.S. was initially intended for all faculty, it has turned out to be especially helpful to new faculty members. Following is an edited version of the survey used at the start of the new program in 1998.

Sharing Our Skills

There are 160 faculty and administrators in XYZ High School. Together, we are a community. In a healthy community such as ours, people help each other grow.

The XYZ High School community is a place where faculty engage in continuous inquiry about our own teaching and learning, as well as about student needs, achievement, and performance; where we seek out opportunities to share insights and expertise; and where we look upon each other as powerful and accessible sources of collegial and professional help and support.

In order to help this process along, the Professional Development Committee plans to publish a listing of those of us interested in making ourselves available to our colleagues for the purpose of sharing professional knowledge and skills. If interested in being part of this collegial opportunity, please complete the following survey and return it to _____ by _____.

Survey

Name, etc._____
    Yes, I am interested in being part of our community of learners by sharing professional expertise, knowledge, skills, and interests with my colleagues.
    I would be willing to participate in activities with interested colleagues in the following area(s). Check all that apply.

_____ Present a brief workshop to an interested group. Please specify subject(s).

```
       _____ Lead an informal discussion group. Please spec-
       ify topic(s).
       _____ Provide specific information or materials to a
       colleague on request. Please specify area(s).

I have these questions, comments, or suggestions:
```

Finally, perhaps the deepest and most long-lasting way veteran teachers can help their new colleagues may simply be by being compassionate listeners and avid cheerleaders.

Mentors

In addition to sharing the responsibility of orienting new teachers to the school, district, and community; assisting in the development of the mentoring program; linking new teachers to resources; and providing new teachers with ongoing emotional as well as professional support, mentors have another, more specific, responsibility and role. A new teacher needs to develop the capacity and confidence to make his or her own informed decisions, enrich his or her own knowledge, and sharpen his or her own abilities regarding teaching and learning—in other words, to become self-reliant. Purposefully bringing a beginning teacher to this level of professionalism is the mentor's primary role.

Some mentoring programs provide a few of their veteran mentor teachers with opportunities for additional responsibilities by offering them the role of lead mentor or membership on committees that interview prospective teachers. James Rowley and Patricia Hart of the University of Dayton, in their *Facilitator's Guide to High Performance Mentoring* (2000), suggest some additional tasks for these teacher leaders:

- Plan and deliver beginning-of-the-school-year orientation programs for entry-year teachers.

- Facilitate mentoring training programs.

- Plan and facilitate mentor teacher support sessions in which mentors have the opportunity to engage in collegial dialogue and problem solving.

- Conduct professional development workshops for entry-year teachers.

- Serve as arbitrators to help resolve conflicts between mentors and mentees.

New Teachers (Mentees)

New teachers can help the mentoring program in general and themselves in particular by (a) participating in the program's evaluation and revision efforts; (b) taking an active role in the mentoring relationship by reflecting on decisions made and the results of those decisions, and sharing those reflections with their mentors; (c) proactively seeking help and support from their mentors and others; (d) seeking out and remaining open to feedback; and (e) taking charge of their own professional development, and applying what is learned to the continuous improvement of teaching and learning in the classroom.

Expecting new teachers to take on all these responsibilities in addition to everything else they face when they begin a teaching career is expecting a lot. They will need support, understanding, patience, and positive reinforcement along the way.

Mentoring Program Coordinator

Management of the mentoring program is not a job for a committee. One person—a mentoring committee member perhaps, or an administrator, mentor teacher, or retired former mentor, someone who is available to mentors and who is accountable to the mentoring committee—can efficiently handle day-to-day issues, provided he or she (a) thoroughly understands everyone's role and responsibility, (b) is clear about the purpose and goals of the program, (c) is familiar with the many aspects of the local school district, and (d) has the authority and resources to do the job.

The mentor program coordinator is the person who protects mentors from the burden of administrative duties. Ideally, he or she has had experience mentoring and dealing with physical arrangements and logistics. The coordinator, among other responsibilities, might schedule the use of meeting rooms; arrange for training, materials, and the use of equipment; monitor activities; keep track of logs, portfolios, journals, and meetings; provide data for program evaluation; and engage in overall problem solving for the good of the program. For example, Carl O'Connell, Mentor Program Coordinator for the Rochester (New York) School District, stresses the importance of interpersonal problem solving. He finds that a significant aspect of his role "is that of troubleshooter—monitoring relationships among mentors, administrators, and interns."

Exercise 4.1 *What Others Can Do*

Retired teachers, students, school board members, parents, and support staff can also have roles in a mentoring program. For example, retired teachers who have time and interest might be trained and serve as mentors.

Soliciting student feedback in terms of what helps and what hinders their learning can provide important data upon which a new teacher can reflect. School board members and parents can serve on planning committees, and advocate for policies and decisions that establish and support a mentoring program.

Support staff can keep records, reproduce documentation, and discuss expectations and roles with mentors and new teachers.

What other ways might these people contribute to a mentoring program?

Retired teachers: _____

_____

_____

Students: _____

_____

_____

School board members: _____

_____

_____

Parents: _____

_____

_____

Support staff: _____

_____

_____

Whatever the roles and responsibilities are determined to be for individuals in your mentoring program, they should be clearly defined and understood from the beginning.

5

Policies, Procedures, and Particulars

After all the mission statements and goal pronouncements have been made, after all the school board's rhetoric of support has become public record, after all is said and done—will more be said than done?

Ultimately, mentoring is done one-on-one within the mentor-mentee relationship. It is the decisions made by the mentoring committee, however, that empower the mentor-mentee relationship to get things done.

The decisions made by the committee must be those that fit the school or district's unique characteristics and needs—one size does *not* fit all! When your committee members are ready to decide on a policy or procedure, here are 10 questions they can ask themselves to determine whether a decision is the right one for their school or district:

1. Why are we making this decision?

2. What could happen if we don't make this decision?

3. What, if anything, will be better because of this decision?

4. What, if anything, will be worse because of this decision?

5. What effect, if any, will making this decision have on people?

6. What effect, if any, will making this decision have on other elements of the mentoring program?

7. What effect, if any, will making this decision have on the school or district's macrosystems?

8. Will it work in the context of the school's or district's policies, budget, and operational structure?

9. Will it work in the context of the school's or district's informal culture?

10. Will it work in the context of the school's or district's professional contracts and agreements?

Things change—and over time, so will the answers to these questions, which is why the mentoring committee must continue to function over time. Once the initial policies, procedures, and particulars are in place (and this can take several years to accomplish), the committee's task will be to keep asking the questions and making modifications dictated by changes in the answers. In essence, the mentoring program is always in its pilot stage.

The balance of this chapter examines the issues faced by most mentoring program committees, and suggests strategies to address them. The nitty-gritty policies, procedures, and particulars your committee develops, implements, and operates are what will give the program its structure.

Most decisions about time, budget, and compensation for mentors are not ones for the mentoring committee to make. They are the prerogative of school board policy, administrative directives, or collective bargaining. The role of the mentoring committee in regard to these issues is (a) to decide what, realistically, would be best for the program, (b) to make recommendations to the appropriate body, and (c) to support their recommendations with statements of purpose, relevant data, and well thought-out plans for implementation and oversight.

Time

Ask a group of mentors and mentees what they consider the biggest barrier to mentoring, and 9 out of 10 (an unresearched estimate) will throw up their hands in frustration and mumble something like, "I never have enough time" or "There aren't enough hours in a day."

How time is used is significant, but having the use of time is crucial. Just as crucial as time is timing. I recently completed a series of mentor training sessions for a group of veteran teachers in a midsized district. The district's negotiated contract provided a generous amount of time for the training (one afternoon a week for 10 weeks). The training began in March and extended through the end of May. The veteran teachers, not yet trained, had been mentoring beginning teachers since the school year began in September. Guess what? Sure, the training developed the mentors' skills, knowledge and understanding about mentoring, but did so (a) too late to do much good for the current year's crop of beginners, and (b) too soon to be able to make meaningful connections with the needs of next year's crop of new teachers. Ideally, training of new mentors should begin toward the end of the summer, extend through the orientation and induction periods for new teachers, and then be spaced throughout the school year in order to reinforce skills, fine-tune strategies, and address evolving needs.

If mentoring is a high enough priority in a school or district, then adequate time and realistic timing must be provided. Professor Mary Anne Raywid (1993) of Hofstra University cautions that "in finding time for substantial, continuing teacher collaboration . . . it is neither fair nor wise to ask teachers to deduct all the time needed from their personal lives (like weekends and holidays), even with compensation." On the other hand, I have found that even when enough time for mentoring is provided, it is not uncommon for a conscientious mentor and mentee to arrange some additional meeting time *on their own*, over lunch, for example, or perhaps for a few minutes before a scheduled faculty meeting. Professor Raywid also cautions—and rightfully so—that "conscientious teachers are reluctant to be away from their classrooms for an extended time unless they can feel confident about what is happening in their absence." Following are a dozen suggestions of ways to provide time for mentor-mentee collaboration:

1. Schedule a mentor and mentee pair for the same lunch period. This provides a daily opportunity for mentor and mentee to briefly touch bases and develop their relationship.

2. Schedule daily preparation periods so that, each week, two are during a period common to both mentor and mentee, and three are at different periods. In this way, mentor and mentee have the opportunity twice a week to schedule time for conferencing and observing each other's class, and still have time to attend to their own individual tasks.

3. Consider multiple mentors. By sharing a mentee with two or more mentors, each mentor can devote less time to the mentee. An added benefit is that mentors have the opportunity to discuss confidential issues concerning the mentee with a committed colleague—an option not normally available.

4. Encourage and support frequent 15-minute mentor-mentee meetings before and after school by providing refreshments and/or by making additional compensation available.

5. Arrange to have mentees' classes videotaped. Mentees will still need face-to-face pre- and postclass conferences with mentors, but videotaping does not require both parties to be present at the time. Pre- and postclass conferences can be scheduled more flexibly than classroom visits, and the tapes can be reviewed at the convenience of the mentor and mentee.

6. Hire a "Supersub," a permanent substitute teacher who gets to know the staff, students, and curriculum. This person's priority is the mentoring program. He or she takes over a mentor's or mentee's class while one is observing the other. Because those observations are scheduled ahead of time, the substitute can be thoroughly prepared to teach the class, and the students will always see the same substitute. It will probably require the cooperation of the teachers' bargaining unit to work out details, such as whether the sub-

stitute accrues length-of-service credit. Even small districts can reasonably expect to need a sub or two most days, so when not involved with mentoring, the person can be available for other substitute duties or can be used as an aide or resource person.

7. Arrange classrooms so that mentors are next to or across the hall from their mentees. This can encourage touching bases more frequently than otherwise.

8. Follow the example of one small elementary school principal who teaches a class once or twice each month for each new teacher while the beginner observes his or her mentor.

9. Provide opportunities in situations where mentor and mentee do not teach in the same building for contact via e-mail and telephone. Although not as effective as face-to-face meetings, doing so can encourage more frequent "base-touching" than might otherwise be the case.

10. Assign first-year teachers and their mentors fewer classes or noninstructional duties, with the understanding that the additional time available will be used for mentoring.

11. Team new teachers with their mentors in schools where teachers teach in teams, thereby creating ideal opportunities for quality mentoring time.

12. Recruit retired teachers or experts from nature centers, museums, or industry to volunteer to present their expertise to a class while the mentor or mentee is away. Because it is generally required that a certified teacher or substitute be in attendance, it may be necessary—even desirable—to combine such a class with another along with its teacher.

There are two decisions about time that *are* within the purview of a mentoring committee. One of these decisions is whether mentors and mentees should be required to meet a given number of times during a given period of time. The answer depends on local situations, of course, but when there is such a requirement, mentors typically receive compensation. Where possible, mentors should meet with their mentees every day or two during the first two weeks, approximately once every week or two for the rest of the first semester, and less often the rest of the year. These meetings should be scheduled in advance and documented, especially if compensation is involved.

The second time-related decision within the purview of the committee concerns how many years a new teacher should be mentored. Conventional wisdom says two years, but some flexibility is prudent. A goal of mentoring is to wean the new teacher away from relying on a mentor for direction and suggestions. The mentor-mentee relationship must not become a parent-child one; the mentor needs to know when to let go. The mentor will have achieved this goal when the mentee demonstrates the willingness and ability to make informed professional decisions autonomously, to act on those decisions with confidence, to reflect on the effectiveness of those actions, and to modify procedures based on thoughtful analysis of accurate data. At this point—whether it occurs during the first year or not until the end of the second or even third year of teaching—a formal mentor-mentee relationship should end and transform into a peer-partnership in which colleagues can function as mentors for each other.

Money

Money buys time. The availability of money will influence the extent to which your program will be able to provide time for mentors and mentees to meet and to observe each other in the classroom. Training mentors costs money, too, as does providing them with materials to help them do their job. The committee needs to be proactive in the development of a mentoring program budget proposal. Following are 10 potential line items to consider:

1. Salaries and/or stipends (more about this in the discussion about compensation)

2. Substitutes (e.g., permanent and/or occasional)

3. Recruiting volunteers (e.g., retired teachers and professionals in other fields)

4. Purchased services (e.g., consultants for such tasks as data collection and analysis, mentor training, and program evaluation)

5. Travel (e.g., visiting programs in other schools)

6. Supplies, material, equipment (e.g., publications, videos, software for a professional resource center; production of forms and mentoring handbooks)

7. Professional conference fees and expenses (e.g., for mentors to attend programs with mentees)

8. Meeting facilities (e.g., occasional off-campus meetings or retreats)

9. Activities for new teachers (e.g., summer orientation programs, "new teacher academy," visits to veteran teachers in other schools)

10. Year-end celebration or recognition of mentors and new teachers

Realistically, it may not always be possible to end up with a budget large enough to support all 10 of the line items suggested above. Therefore it would be helpful to prioritize the budget items you would like to include so that available funds can be allocated effectively.

Trying to prioritize even 4 or 5 items, let alone 10 or more, can be difficult. I sometimes use a process called "paired comparison" to prioritize a list of items. I first learned of the paired comparison process from "A Creative Approach to Evaluating Ideas," by Robert J. Gillespie (1972).

The gist of the process is to list the items being considered, and then weigh each item against each of the others, one pair at a time. The idea behind the process is that you need to decide the relative importance between only two items at a time rather than all at once. Here is an example of how paired comparison works. Suppose I want to

- Buy a new textbook series
- Replace some equipment
- Provide some specialized professional development for teachers

Each item will cost the same amount. My budget only allows me to buy one now, one next month, and one in two months. I want to prioritize the list.

First, I weigh the need for textbooks against equipment. Considering such criteria as the effect of delay on program and people, I decide that if I could buy only one item on the list today, it would be equipment. That's one vote for equipment.

Then, using the same criteria, I compare textbooks and professional development. Let's say I choose professional development. That's one for equipment, one for professional development—so far.

Now, it's equipment versus professional development. My choice is for equipment.

The final score and priority in descending order of importance is

- Equipment (two votes)
- Professional development (one vote)
- Textbooks (no votes)

Exercise 5.1 Prioritize Budget Line Items

Using the paired comparison process and keeping your particular mentoring program in mind, prioritize the following budget line items.

Line Item	Which Is More Important?	Decision
Stipends	Stipends vs. substitutes	
	Stipends vs. recruiting	
	Stipends vs. services	
	Stipends vs. travel	
	Stipends vs. supplies	
	Stipends vs. conference fees	
	Stipends vs. meeting facilities	
	Stipends vs. activities	
	Stipends vs. celebration	
Substitutes	Substitutes vs. recruiting	
	Substitutes vs. services	
	Substitutes vs. travel	
	Substitutes vs. supplies	
	Substitutes vs. conference fees	
	Substitutes vs. meeting facilities	
	Substitutes vs. activities	
	Substitutes vs. celebration	
Recruiting	Recruiting vs. services	
	Recruiting vs. travel	
	Recruiting vs. supplies	
	Recruiting vs. conference fees	
	Recruiting vs. meeting facilities	
	Recruiting vs. activities	
	Recruiting vs. celebration	

Exercise 5.1 (continued)

Line Item	Which Is More Important?	Decision
Services	Services vs. travel	
	Services vs. supplies	
	Services vs. conference fees	
	Services vs. meeting facilities	
	Services vs. activities	
	Services vs. celebration	
Travel	Travel vs. supplies	
	Travel vs. conference fees	
	Travel vs. meeting facilities	
	Travel vs. activities	
	Travel vs. celebration	
Supplies	Supplies vs. conference fees	
	Supplies vs. meeting facilities	
	Supplies vs. activities	
	Supplies vs. celebration	
Conference fees	Conference fees vs. meeting facilities	
	Conference fees vs. activities	
	Conference fees vs. celebration	
Meeting facilities	Meeting facilities vs. activities	
	Meeting facilities vs. celebration	
Activities	Activities vs. celebration	

Now, add up the number of times that each item won the decision. Arrange the decisions in numerical order: This is your priority order.

Many states offer financial aid in addition to grants to help districts start new teacher induction/mentoring programs. In California, for example, the Beginning Teacher Support and Assessment Program (BTSAP) became a permanent state initiative in 1992 run jointly by the state's education department and the Commission on Teacher Credentialing. For approved districts, the BTSAP recommends $5,000 be budgeted for each new teacher—the state contributes $3,000, with the other $2,000 to be provided locally. Check periodically with your state Department of Education for the availability of grants or other funding opportunities for mentoring programs.

Compensation

Providing some form of compensation not only helps attract and retain quality mentors, it also signals that the school or district values and recognizes the work of the mentor. According to the AFT's *Educational Issues Policy Brief* (1998), several states provide funding that is specifically allowable for mentor stipends.

Another example of an alternative source of funds for compensation is a 1995 provision by the New Jersey Department of Education that allows a mentor, in exchange for providing "training, support, and evaluation," to receive a $500 stipend, which is to be deducted from the new teacher's salary over the course of the school year. Yet another example is the 1998 offer by the Massachusetts Department of Education to award a $5,000 bonus to teachers who hold certification from the National Board for Professional Teaching Standards (NBPTS) and are trained and serve as a mentors to a new teachers.

AFT and the NEA agree in their 1998 jointly produced handbook, *Peer Assistance & Peer Review*, that

> given the demanding nature of the work and the expertise and training that is required, [mentors] should be properly compensated for their services [and] both the structure and level of compensation need to be determined jointly by the local affiliate and the school district in conformity with collective bargaining agreements.

Contractual language usually specifies that mentor stipends be in addition to salary. The Los Angeles Contract (Article XXVI, section 8.1), for example, states that these stipends "shall not be counted as salaries or wages for State Teachers' Retirement System purposes." Incidentally, the Pittsburgh contract authorizes an expense stipend for newly hired teachers of $35 per day for the official orientation day(s). The San Francisco contract requires that the mentoring program "shall remain operative as long as there are state funds allocated for the Mentor Teacher Program or if the School Board appropriates other funds."

Compensation can also be provided in forms other than monetary. For example,

- Tuition waivers for graduate work
- Release time for professional development and consultation
- A reduced course load or reduced number of preparations
- Perks, such as a reserved parking space, a laptop computer, or home Internet access
- Release from noninstructional duties, such as chaperoning, hall or lunch duty, or recess
- End-of-year recognition dinner, certificates, plaques, and so forth
- Continuing Education Units (CEUs) or Professional Development Points (PDPs) toward recertification requirements and/or pay scale upgrades
- Vouchers for subscriptions to professional journals
- Small grants for professional development activities or additional classroom materials

The mentoring committee does have responsibility for making decisions in the areas discussed in this chapter, most of which can be assembled, along with a board of education policy and relevant contract sections, in a mentoring manual or handbook, and distributed to all mentors and new teachers. Such a compendium should be in a format that allows for easy revision and updating—a loose-leaf binder, for example.

Selection of Mentors

A school administrator posted this message recently on a beginning teacher Internet chat board: "Our school district is trying to develop a mentoring program for new teachers. We would love to hear from teachers involved in such a program, especially from new teachers. . . . What advice can you give us?" Here, *verbatim*, is the reply from a person signing himself/herself "a mentoree."

> I am a first-year teacher who was given a mentor. My mentor was someone I had met and talked to and liked very much. However, once she volunteered to be my mentor things changed for the worse. At first I thought she was just socially awkward. For example, after observing my class we would talk about strengths and weaknesses. But she came across as if there was only one way to

teach—her way—and all others were wrong. She did not talk to me as a peer, but as someone who thought that they were the perfect teacher, and all others paled in comparison. However, that was something I could handle. After all I know I am a good teacher and I love what I do. What bothers me about my "mentor" is the jealousy. Once she started hearing compliments that I would get she stopped being helpful. In some instances she was downright cold and aloof. I guess my advice is *choose your mentors wisely.* (italics added)

The advice given by this anonymous first-year teacher is critical—so critical, in fact, that the selection of mentors must not be considered merely a matter of convenience and availability. One of the first and most basic decisions to be made by the mentoring committee is the criteria and process for recruiting and selecting mentors. Even very small programs with limited options will benefit from establishing a list of characteristics deemed desirable in a mentor.

There is no fixed rule that governs what traits or circumstances are most important when it comes to selecting mentors, except that the criteria should be based on the goals and needs of the local program. Most of those who select mentors consider highly those veteran teachers who have expertise and credibility in the classroom. Classroom expertise by itself, however, does not guarantee effective and accomplished performance as a mentor of adults. Monica Janas (1996) of University of Charleston School of Education cites research that indicates "the most frequently mentioned characteristic of effective mentors is a willingness to nurture another person." Professor Janas goes on to suggest that "it is also beneficial to seek individuals as mentors who are people-oriented, open-minded, flexible, and empathetic. Collaborative and cooperative skills are particularly crucial social skills as are qualities of receptiveness, responsiveness, openness, and dependability."

In addition to the elements of character, attitude, and interpersonal skills desirable in mentors, lists of qualities and abilities often stipulate that candidates are certified, have taught successfully for a specified number of years, demonstrate knowledge of the subjects they teach, possess a wide repertoire of effective classroom management and instructional strategies, reflect the diverse population of the teaching staff, and understand the politics and culture of the school community.

There are several ways to assess the qualities of a potential mentor: application forms; interviews; recommendations from or informal conversations with teachers, administrators, students, support staff, and parents; records of professional activities and presentations; professional portfolios; and observations or videotapes of classroom teaching.

Because ideal candidates may not automatically apply to become mentors, it is a good idea to recruit them. For example, here are excerpts from a speech to faculty, presented in early June, by the chairperson of a school district's—let's call it the XYZ School District—mentoring program committee.

> Through the generous service of individuals over the past five years, teachers new to the XYZ School District have enjoyed the benefits of friendly, professional orientation and ongoing assistance in developing their craft as teachers. I want to take this opportunity to thank the following dedicated faculty members who served as mentors in the past year: Mr. Smith, . . .
>
> Next year we will welcome 27 new faculty members. I invite any teacher who has four or more years of professional experience—at least two in the XYZ District—and some confidence in your craft to consider serving next year as a mentor. You don't have to be "Superteacher"! We're all in this together and all still learning.
>
> If you are interested in serving as a mentor and would like more details, please see me or any member of the mentoring committee during the coming week. [Members of the committee were then introduced, and their names, locations, and phone numbers were listed in a brochure given to faculty.]
>
> Why be a mentor? Mentoring is an opportunity to help induct a new colleague into the profession we value. In addition, those who mentor often report that the relationship enhances their own sense of professionalism and underscores that they are valued for their experience and expertise. Mentoring will also fulfill the district's contractual requirement that each teacher serve on some academic committee or study group at least once every four years.
>
> Although our mentoring program may be considered a routine part of our school culture, as you know, nothing "routine" happens routinely without hard work and commitment.
>
> Thank you for considering this invitation.

Once the mentoring committee has decided upon criteria and eligibility requirements for becoming a mentor, and has determined that all elements of the selection process are compatible with local conditions, state and local regulations, and the mentoring program's goals and objectives, then the criteria should be published and distributed. Publication can be as part of a mentoring handbook and, if appropriate, as an article in a negotiated contract.

Mentor Training

Just because your committee has selected outstanding classroom teachers who meet all the criteria, there is no guarantee that they will be outstanding—or even effective—mentors. It is the *quality* of the mentoring that will determine the extent to which teacher performance and commitment are improved. Mentoring adults is different from teaching children. A dedicated, experienced teacher of children becomes an effective and accomplished mentor of adults by design and training, not by chance.

At a minimum, mentors must be able (a) to build and maintain relationships with their mentees based on mutual trust, respect, and professionalism; (b) to gather and diagnose data about their mentees' ways of teaching and learning; (c) to coach and conference with their mentees in ways that help them fine-tune their professional skills, enhance their grasp of subject matter, and locate and acquire resources; (d) to expand their mentees' repertoire of teaching modalities; and (e) to wean their mentees away from dependence by guiding them through the process of reflecting on decisions and actions for themselves while encouraging them to construct their own informed teaching and learning approaches.

There are several publications that provide comprehensive information, materials, handouts, and suggested activities for training mentors. I have found the following to be among the most useful.

Mentoring: A Resource and Training Guide for Educators, by Anne Newton et al. (1994): This comprehensive training guide for mentoring was developed by staff from state education agencies in Maine, Massachusetts, New Hampshire, New York, and Vermont, and staff from The Regional Laboratory for Educational Improvement of the Northeast and Islands. Eight school districts piloted the material in the 800-page guidebook and provided feedback for its modification.

Mentoring to Improve Schools, by Barry Sweeny and Todd Johnson (1999): This facilitator's guide, which contains several workshop designs with supporting handouts and overheads, is supplemented by two videos.

High Performance Mentoring, by James Rowley and Patricia Hart (2000): This multimedia package provides an integrated and progressive series of 25 training modules that incorporate videotapes, a CD-ROM with PowerPoint® slides, a participant's notebook, and a facilitator's guide.

Mentoring New Teachers, by Hal Portner (1998): This book provides comprehensive discussions, examples, and activities for individuals interested in developing basic mentoring behaviors.

Another Set of Eyes, by Acheson, K., Costa, A., & Garmston, R. (1989): This set of five videotapes with two trainer's manuals demonstrates techniques for classroom observation and conferencing skills.

When you select a trainer, ask questions that elicit the extent of the person's understanding of the four mentoring functions and how she or he will address them in the training sessions. For example, you can ask,

"What, in your opinion, does a mentor of new teachers need to know and be able to do?" and "How do you propose to develop these traits or behaviors in the people being trained?" You should feel comfortable and confident about the trainer's experience, expertise, and ability to relate well with your mentors. The trainer is, after all, a mentor of mentors, and should meet such a set of criteria. The best time for training to begin is in the late summer, so that mentors are ready from day one of the new school year to "hit the ground running."

Matching Mentors and Mentees

Beginning teachers are a diverse group. Some are just entering adulthood. Others are mature adults who left another profession for teaching. There are also "experienced beginners," teachers new to a school or district who are reentering the profession after raising a family or who taught in another school or district the previous year. Consequently, age and previous experience can be factors to consider when pairing mentor and mentee. In some instances, a common gender, ethnic, or cultural match may be advantageous.

There is general agreement that the match most likely to succeed is the one where mentor and mentee teach the same subject at the same grade level in the same building, and have ready access to each other's classroom. It must be noted again, however, that even where proximity dictates a particular match, it is the *quality* of the relationship that could make or break its effectiveness. Some programs, rather than administratively assigning mentors to new teachers, have a pool of trained mentors who meet with the group of new teachers during their orientation to socialize, share teaching philosophies, discuss the mentoring process, and voluntarily form tentative mentor-mentee pairs. If such a relationship falters, changes can be made after reservations are expressed to a mentor coordinator and agreement reached by all parties concerned.

In some schools and districts, supply and demand present a challenge. Not only is it impossible in such a situation to match a mentor and mentee in the same discipline or building, but there are not even enough mentors available to assign to all the new teachers. Hiring retired teachers as mentors may help.

Another fairly common scenario is one in which the people who want to be mentors are the same people who are active in other professional activities and committees. In spite of their dedication, they can only do so much. The NFIE (1999) suggests one possible solution:

> [Abandon] the traditional model of matching a protégé to a single mentor in favor of matching a protégé to several different mentors, each of whom offers assistance in various specialized areas, such as grade-level and/or subject-matter expertise, the use of technol-

ogy, classroom management, and everyday questions involving policies, politics, and procedures.

Finally, you might want to produce a version of the following form letter for mentors to send once they have been assigned a mentee.

```
Dear Colleague,

My name is _____. I teach _____
at _____. Welcome to _____
School/District.

I am a trained mentor teacher who has been assigned to
assist you during your first year or two of teaching. I
want you to think of me as a resource person and coach. I
will not in any way evaluate you. Our time together will
be held in the strictest confidence.
   Some of the areas we might explore together are the
culture and policies of the school and district, class-
room management, curriculum, student assessment, lesson
planning, instructional strategies, opportunities for
professional growth, and any other topics that you re-
quest.
   I will arrange to meet with you as soon as possible
to discuss the mentoring program and to set a mutually
convenient schedule for future meetings. Meanwhile, if
you need to contact me, please (call, e-mail, leave a
message, etc.) at _____.
   Again, I look forward to meeting and working with
you.

Sincerely,
(Mentor Teacher)
```

Monitoring

There needs to be some system of monitoring mentors and their activities. Those who support the program deserve to have evidence that mentors are carrying out their roles and responsibilities—at least in terms of time on task and other such quantitative data—and that their support of the program is generating some useful results. However, beyond providing material for program accountability, the value of monitoring mentors and documenting their activities lies in the opportunity it provides for support, reflection, and adjustment.

Generally, programs maintain records of numbers of participants and the amount of time spent in program activities. Keeping in mind that a reasonable effort needs to be made to minimize paperwork, a program policy might call for mentors to meet with mentees for specific amounts and intervals of time for specific purposes, and to document compliance with that requirement. Some procedural policies may require mentors to produce an action plan with their mentee and submit a reflection paper based on its results. Still others may ask mentors to set goals and time-lines, develop action plans for themselves, and meet with their peers for support and periodic progress reports.

The principal of an elementary school in Arizona gives each of her mentors at the beginning of the school year a notebook to journal in, be-cause, as she says, "We are so committed to writing and reflection, and I think reflection is a huge part of good mentoring." Mentors in a district in South Carolina each receive a locally produced "Mentor Reflective Log" in which they are requested to record the dates, topics, and performance dimensions discussed with their mentees, and to reflect on those meet-ings with an emphasis on the effectiveness of their own performance. Finally, be sure to check with the local teachers' bargaining unit to clarify any perception of conflict such documentation requirements may have vis-à-vis the negotiated contract.

When to Intervene

What does a mentor do when the physical or emotional safety of children is in jeopardy as a result of the mentoring program or process? Does the mentor share this information with the principal? What about the funda-mental tenet of confidentially in the mentoring process? In the medical profession, doctors take the Hippocratic oath, which begins, "First, do no harm. . . . " I believe the same holds true for educators. Although we all may make mistakes when learning, the right of a mentee learning to be a better teacher or of an experienced teacher learning to mentor does not in-clude the right to harm children in the process. The mentoring committee should formulate and distribute a policy specifying when and how to in-tervene when it is determined that the actions of a mentor or mentee threaten someone's physical or emotional health, safety, or right to an equal educational opportunity.

Other Decisions to Contemplate

Frequency of Mentor-Mentee Meetings

Should the program dictate how often and for what length of time mentors and mentees meet? This is usually the case where mentors re-ceive compensation, and where accountability is therefore necessary. Otherwise, consider leaving those decisions up to the mentors, and per-haps have them log and reflect on those meetings (see *Monitoring* on page 68).

The Nature of Mentor-Mentee Meetings

Should the program establish a mentoring curriculum? A well-trained mentor should be able to assess the needs of her or his mentee, and plan accordingly. However, if the committee feels the need to provide some direction to the mentoring process, it should be done only on a general category basis, with plenty of room for adjustment to individual situations. Certainly, it is not the role of the committee to micromanage the mentor-mentee relationship.

Required or Voluntary Participation

Should all newly hired teachers be required to work with a mentor? What about teachers new to your school or district who are not beginning teachers? As a codicil, you may want to plan for situations where a one-on-one match cannot be made (e.g., where there are not enough trained mentors or where no mentor is available in a particular subject area). The section on *Matching Mentors and Mentees* on page 67 suggests some ways around such a predicament.

Professional Development for Newly Trained Mentors

Allow me to make a couple of assumptions about newly certified teachers.

- Most newly certified teachers know the theory and understand the principles of the profession, but have yet to apply them effectively in the classroom.

- Ignoring the need of new teachers for ongoing professional development can adversely affect the ability of their students to learn, and may contribute to the teachers leaving the profession prematurely.

Now, here are parallel assumptions about newly trained mentors.

- Newly trained mentors, like newly certified teachers, have acquired skills and understandings, but may not be able to apply them effectively in authentic settings.

- Leaving the ongoing professional development of mentors to chance can jeopardize their effectiveness, contribute to their dissatisfaction with the process, and ultimately lead to the demise of the entire mentoring program.

Once mentors have been initially trained, your program's next step—should you agree with my assumptions—is to help them get better at what they do. Although it may be appropriate in some instances, I do not advocate limiting this help—let's call it "professional development"—for previously trained mentors solely to skill development and theory acquisition in workshop settings. Rather, I advocate the kinds of activities that (a) encourage mentors to identify, grapple with, and address their own limitations as mentors, and (b) help them discover, adapt, and develop practices that work best for them in their own particular settings and situations.

Principles of Professional Development for Trained Mentors

Judith Warren Little (1993), University of California, Berkeley, posits several principles that move professional development beyond the ubiquitous workshop model. Although Professor Little formulated these principles with teachers in mind, we can, based on our assumptions about the similarities between new teachers and new mentors, consider some of them as germane to the professional development of newly trained mentors. Here are five of her principles and my commentary on how professional development for practicing mentors might reasonably be tested against them.

1. Professional development offers meaningful intellectual, social, and emotional engagement with ideas, with materials, and with colleagues both in and out of [the teaching profession].

This principle recognizes that professional development can be job embedded and that professional interactions occurring outside of formal workshop settings are legitimate professional development activities. It encourages mentors to observe, consult with, and collaborate with other mentors and mentees both in and out of the public school milieu. It says, for example, that it is okay—even desirable—to investigate mentoring in other settings, such as universities, industry, and the community at large.

2. Professional development takes explicit account of the context of [mentoring] and the experience of [mentors].

Adherence to this principle encourages mentors not only to learn something new or to enhance what they already know, but also to gain an understanding of how their new learning relates to their own particular settings and situations. Implicit in this principle is the challenge to invent new ways to apply theory to practice.

3. Professional development offers support for informed dissent.

This principle emphasizes critical thinking. It places a premium on the evaluation of alternatives and the close scrutiny of underlying assumptions. It furthers the intent of Principle 2 by stressing that "one size may not fit all" when it comes to applying a mentoring behavior or concept in a particular situation or context. It also implies that long-term inquiry, as opposed to "one-shot" presentations, provides opportunity for the development of the kind of thoughtful, principled, and well-informed dissent that strengthens decisions.

4. Professional development places [mentoring] practice in the larger contexts of school practice.

This principle reminds us to connect the content and process of professional development for mentors with the big picture. It challenges mentors to understand the interrelationship of mentoring to the rest of the educational community and to see mentoring as more than just the application of a set of technical skills.

5. *Professional development prepares [mentors] to employ the techniques and perspectives of inquiry.*

Without denying that training mentors in the skills and behaviors of mentoring is essential, this principle acknowledges the value of pursuing knowledge for its own sake. It reminds us that our existing knowledge base is relatively slim, and that we would be well served not only by accessing knowledge claimed by others, but also by constructing our own.

Mentors Must Take Charge of Their Own Ongoing Professional Development

Some mentors will be constantly searching for new and better ways. Others will be burnt out. Most will be somewhere in between. Professional development can benefit them all, provided that the mentors take responsibility for their own professional development. The role of the mentoring program is to provide the opportunity, encouragement, support, and resources. Here are some suggestions.

Identify an Area of Focus

Schedule a session for mentors during which they ask themselves, "What more do I need to know and be able to do in order to better help my mentees achieve what *they* need to know and be able to do?" Prior to the session, send each participant a brief summary of what the session is about. For example, you might send a letter like the following.

```
Dear Colleague:

As discussed during last month's mentor group meeting,
we will get together on [date] from [time] to [time] at
[place] to begin the process of taking charge of our own
professional development. The objective of this meeting
is to identify an area of focus for our professional de-
velopment that we consider to be important enough for us
to devote our time and energy to pursue. Although some
of you may want to work on this independently, I suggest
you work in pairs or small groups where you can bounce
ideas off of one another.

    You can prepare for the meeting in several ways.
First you should review and reflect on your journal
writings to see if there are areas where there may be a
difference between the way your mentoring experience is
going and the way you would like it to be. Second, read
```

the enclosed article, "The Good Mentor," by James B.
Rowley. Finally, you need to complete the enclosed self-
assessment.

Bring your thoughts, your journal, and the enclosed
materials with you. Hopefully, the outcome of the meeting will be the identification of areas that you consider to be the year's focus of professional development as
a mentor.

Sincerely,

(Mentor Coordinator)

Enclosures (2)

One of the enclosures I referred to in the above sample letter was "The
Good Mentor," an article by James B. Rowley from the May 1999 issue of
Educational Leadership (pp. 20–22). In the article, Rowley identifies
"six basic but essential qualities of the *good mentor* and the implications
the qualities have for entry-year program design and mentor teacher
training."

The other enclosure is a self-assessment. Rather than constructing
such an assessment in the usual checklist format, I recommend using a series of open-ended questions in order to stimulate reflection. Here are
some suggestions:

1. What was one of the most successful mentoring sessions I conducted? What made it so successful?

2. What was one of the most stressful mentoring sessions I conducted? What made it so difficult?

3. If I had to describe, in one sentence, my major strength as a mentor, what would I say?

4. If I had to describe my major shortcoming as a mentor, what
   would I say?

5. What do I know about my mentees as individuals that helps me
   mentor them effectively?

6. Which of my mentoring methods is strongest? Weakest?

7. Do I know enough about recent research and new practices in my
   subject area in order to keep my mentee up to date?

8. If I had time and resources, what additional mentoring-related
   project would I like to try? What would I need to know and be able
   to do in order to carry out such a project?

9. What does the data I've collected tell me about my mentees in
   terms of what they need to know and be able to do? What more do
   I need to know and be able to do in order to help them?

10. In my role as a mentor, to what extent do I effectively
    - Use supplementary material?
    - Use technology?
    - Use resource persons and community resources?

11. What, if any, new or revised curriculum, technology, or process is being planned for our district that my mentees should know more about, and, if any are, do I know enough about it myself?

Remember, the purpose of the meeting is to identify areas of focus for the professional development of mentors, both individually and collectively. Here is a segment of a conversation that Gary and Margaret, two teacher mentors, had as they worked together on this task.

Gary: As I read over Rowley's description of a good mentor as one who is "accepting of the beginning teacher," and reflected on just how helpful I was being to my mentee, I realized that sometimes I lose patience when he doesn't understand something.

Margaret: Give me an example. What doesn't he understand?

Gary: Well, when a planned teaching strategy isn't working, he doesn't try something else—and when I point this out to him, he just gives me a blank stare. To make matters worse, the same thing happens over and over. Sometimes I feel as though I'm just spinning my wheels.

Margaret: It sounds like he's just not confident or experienced enough to make "on-the-fly" adjustments to his lesson plan.

They continue to discuss Gary's concern for a while, then he asks Margaret to share her reflections.

Margaret: It's exasperating! I had a mentee last year who couldn't write a lesson plan if her life depended on it, so I spent hours working with my current mentee on lesson plans only to find out that she has been good at it all along.

Gary: Yes, it seems that each beginning teacher is different.

Margaret: It would sure save a lot of time and energy if we could figure out in a hurry just what a mentee needs from us.

By the end of the meeting, Gary decided to focus his individualized professional development as a mentor on learning the developmental stages of a teacher and how to guide a mentee through those stages. Margaret identified the assessment of a mentee's needs as her individual area of focus. They both agreed they needed to know more about how to help mentees not only develop their teaching skills, but also develop their confidence. Most of the other mentors in the meeting agreed that they needed to learn ways to help mentees develop confidence, and this became the group's area of focus.

Find or Create Activities to Address the Focus

The next step for each individual is to develop a set of activities to address his or her area of focus, and for the group to do the same for its area.

Gary, you recall, wanted to know more about the developmental stages of a teacher and how to guide a mentee through those stages. He started with an Internet search engine, using key words and phrases such as "mentoring new teachers," "developmental stages," and "adult development." Then he asked other mentors in his district and on the Internet for models and suggestions. This led to the creation of an informal series of chat room sessions that became a forum for mentors to discuss issues and to network. Gary was enrolled in a doctoral program in a local university, and found a course that related to his focus as well as his program of study.

Margaret's focus was on ways to assess a mentee's needs. She spoke first with Nan, the district's director of professional development, to see how she assessed needs. As a result of that conversation, Margaret expanded her area of focus to include a study of how people took in and processed information. She read material on how to word a questionnaire, reviewed some existing forms, and developed and tested some of her own. She also attended a workshop series on Neuro-Linguistic Programming (NLP) that dealt with ways to assess whether a person was operating in a visual, auditory, or feeling mode at any given time.

Gary and Margaret continued to touch bases regarding the progress of their professional development activities. They found that other small groups of mentors were doing the same. All agreed that the process not only kept them motivated, but also helped mentors create new approaches not only to mentoring, but also to other areas of their professional life. They called the process "peer development."

The mentoring committee honored the group's request to sponsor a workshop for them on motivation and confidence building. The committee also added some material on the subject to the district's professional library, and scheduled workshops over the next two years on the following topics:

- Stage theory and stages of concern
- Adult development and learning styles
- Reflection and journal writing
- Cross-cultural mentoring
- Time and stress management
- Conflict negotiation

- Classroom observation techniques
- Mentoring experienced teachers

There are a number of additional steps one can consider taking when planning for professional development.

Consider Sequencing

Before diving headlong into activities, think about sequencing. Once you have chosen your area of focus, you may want to determine what piece or pieces of that focus you should tackle first. The object here is to isolate a specific aspect of the focus that you feel will have an initial impact on the area and that will form the foundation for subsequent activities.

One way to approach this task is first to consider the gaps that need to be filled in your own abilities, knowledge, skills, and approaches and/or in the particular environment or situation. Then arrange these gaps or needs into a logical order of increasing sophistication.

For example, if Gary, in the above vignette, wasn't familiar with using an Internet search engine, he should learn that skill before diving headlong into his research.

Consider Outcomes

Outcomes are statements of the condition or situation you expect will exist when the need identified as an area of focus has been successfully addressed. Here are five principles for stating an outcome:

1. Make it measurable and observable.
2. Check your motivation. An outcome should express what you really want and should be something you are willing to work for.
3. Establish a deadline, otherwise your outcome is likely to be deferred.
4. Be sure your outcome is realistic, otherwise you may become frustrated and give up.
5. Make your outcome challenging. It should stretch your mind and energies, otherwise you may lose interest.

Here is an example of an outcome statement: *"By the start of the next school year, I will have located, analyzed, and tested at least four instruments and/or techniques for assessing adult learning styles, and selected those appropriate to use with my mentees."*

Consider Problems and Solutions

Anticipate potential barriers to the accomplishment of your outcomes. Then consider what you might do to avoid or surmount those barriers. As you consider possible problems and solutions, you may begin to identify some of the activities or tasks you will want to undertake. You will also find that some of these problems may never occur, simply because they have been anticipated and thus avoided. This is the "preventive maintenance" feature of your planning.

For example, Gary's home computer does not have Internet access, and the ones in school that do are not accessible during his free periods. One solution? The public library.

What are some barriers, points of resistance, interruptions, or obstacles that you might encounter as you implement your plan? How might you avoid or deal with those problems? Use the space below to write your anticipated problems and their possible solutions.

Problem	*Solution*

Consider Resources

Believe it or not, there is a lot of help out there. Your colleagues, the Internet, and the mentoring program coordinator, of course, are major resources. Identify other resources you will need to help you address your area of focus. Consider community, students, other districts, universities, publications, local business, government, professional organizations, regional and state education agencies, family, and friends as potential resources.

What resources can you draw upon for suggestions, materials, and information? Now that you know your area of focus and have clear outcome statements, go on a treasure hunt for resources! List potential resources in the space provided.

Potential resources: _____

_____

_____

_____

_____

_____

_____

Consider Costs

Some of the activities you plan to undertake may involve the expenditure of money. You should know before you start what, if any, financial commitment will be involved for yourself or your school or district.

In the space below, itemize the expenses you expect to incur for each activity. Consider for example fees, travel, meals, supplies, and materials. Determine which expenses you will assume and those for which you will request support.

Costs: _____

_____

_____

_____

_____

Consider Benefits

As a professional educator, you are aware of the value of learning for its own sake. However, you will want to know what positive outcomes to expect as a result of achieving your outcomes.

What's in it for you, not only as a professional, but also as a person? What's in it for the school and district, your colleagues and students? When your outcomes have been accomplished, how will all concerned be better off than before? List below the benefits (tangible and intangible) you can expect as the result of achieving your outcomes.

Benefits: _____

_____

_____

_____

_____

Look to MoM for Help

Another way to provide professional development for newly trained mentors is to arrange for the services of a Mentor of Mentors (MoM). MoM can be an experienced mentor—actively teaching or retired—from your own or a neighboring school or district, a college of education professor, or an education consultant. Whoever assumes the MoM role must be well versed not only in the intricacies of mentoring *per se*, but also experienced in leading study groups of adult professionals.

MoM is more of a coach or guide than a trainer or facilitator. In essence, MoM's interaction with mentors mirrors the mentor-mentee model, except that the content has to do with improving ways to mentor adult colleagues rather than improving ways to teach school-age children.

MoM's work is predominately with the school's or district's cadre of mentors as a group. MoM works with individual mentors when there is a need for confidentiality or in order to observe them interacting with their mentees. MoM also helps members of the group learn from each other by having them assume the role of peer mentor.

One of MoM's initial tasks would be to assess the needs and characteristics of the group, and to structure activities accordingly. For example, if most mentors have already established solid relationships with their mentees, little other than occasional reinforcement is needed in this area. On the other hand, fine-tuning of post-classroom observation conferencing skills might be in order when the mentors are finding it difficult to provide feedback.

MoM's responsibility is to stimulate the mentors' creative and critical thinking, empower them to envision future situations, encourage them to take informed risks, and help them build the capacity to make perceptive decisions and take appropriate actions.

Manage Professional Development Time

Mentors will find it helpful to apply the following effective time management techniques as they carry out their professional development activities:

- Cultivate the habit of including your current activity on your daily or weekly to-do list.

- Assign a high priority to the accomplishment of your activities.

- If an activity will take several hours to complete and you don't have that large a block of time available on a given day, plan to spend only 10 or 15 minutes on that task each day or two. By the end of a week or two, you will have completed the activity.

- You may find it necessary along the way to modify, add to, or omit certain activities. By all means, do so; but be careful not to compromise its basic intent and integrity in the process.

If your mentoring committee decides to provide ongoing professional development opportunities for already trained mentors, they will find the time and energy they devote to the effort to be a wise investment. However, providing the opportunity for professional development is of value only to the extent to which it is used. Ultimately, it is up to individual mentors to seize the opportunity and take charge of their own professional development.

7

Evaluating the Fledgling Mentoring Program

☐ You are shopping in the local market one day in late April when someone taps you on the shoulder. "So, (Mr. or Ms.) Mentoring Program Advocate," says a familiar voice. You turn around; it's Fran Smith, the school board chairperson. "How's the program going? This is its first full year of operation since the committee was formed, right?"

"Yes, this is the program's first year," you answer, "and everything is moving along as planned."

"Glad to hear it. I'm putting you on the board's next agenda. We would like you to update us in on the program's progress and fill us in on what you have planned for next year."

Once the mild shock has worn off, you think to yourself, *"Well, the good news is that they are interested in the mentoring program. The bad news is that we don't have solid statistics yet about the effect the program has had on teacher retention and student learning. That is probably not what they want to hear, but our program just got under way—it's too soon to know."*

You are right on both counts: (a) it is great that the board is interested, and (b) it is too soon to have acquired significant evidence about the program's effect on teacher retention and student learning.

This chapter deals with the reality of evaluating a newly developed mentoring program, a pilot program, and perhaps an older program that has recently taken on a more focused purpose or overhauled its structure. Because we are concerned with new programs, there is not much we can say about a program's past. The purpose of our evaluation will be to understand its present and invent its future.

Oh, and another thing: This chapter is *not* about doing quantitative research. We won't be concerned here with setting up control and experimental groups, conceptualizing independent and dependent variables, or reporting results using inferential statistics.

Now, don't get me wrong: The analysis of quantitative research can define a local program in important ways and contribute to the growing body of knowledge about mentoring—laudable reasons to do that kind of research. Quantitative research, however, is best deferred to the time when your program has matured to the extent that it has a history and has attained outcomes subject to objective delineation and statistical analysis. So, if your program has clear goals and objectives, is well structured, has been in existence for four or more years, and the program committee and school board are interested in such things as the correlation of mentoring to teacher retention, or the effect of mentoring on student achievement, then, by all means, study some publications that touch on objective research methodology (e.g., *Evaluator's Handbook,* Herman, 1987; or *Practical Research, 7th Edition,* Leedy, 2001), then contact a professional researcher.

Why Evaluate?

There are two compelling reasons to evaluate new programs: for accountability and for improvement.

Evaluate a new program for *accountability* to determine whether the program is reaching those whom it was designed to reach, and is doing so in appropriate ways and times. Once a program has been in existence for three or more years, evaluation for accountability can also look at such factors as impact on school culture and effect on student learning.

Evaluate for *improvement* to determine what is not working the way it is supposed to and why. Although there is some overlap between the two reasons for evaluating a program, let's look first at accountability.

Evaluating a New Program for Accountability

Policy- and decision-makers—taxpayers, boards of education, administrators, teacher association leaders, and funding agencies—want data that will help them determine whether the fledgling program should be continued as is, expanded, cut back, or cut out. They are looking for evidence that the program is addressing its objectives and achieving desired outcomes—and they want to be assured that they are getting their money's worth in the process.

On another level, those closer to day-to-day operation and oversight of the program—mentoring program committee members, program coordinators, instructional and curriculum supervisors, building principals, mentors, and mentees—also want to be assured that "all systems are go," that everyone is doing what they are expected to do, and that they are doing it when and how they are supposed to.

The type of information to gather in order to address these needs for accountability are *baseline data* and *initial outcomes*.

Baseline Data

For programs in their first or second years, evaluation for accountability can reasonably expect to assemble demographics and document program implementation. If you have not already done so, now would be a good time to develop the habit of collecting baseline data as soon as they become available so that you can construct both a snapshot of the present and the basis for comparisons later on.

Exercise 7.1 *Your Program's Baseline Data and Their Implications*

Number of new hires who are first-year teachers: _____

Number of new hires who are experienced teachers: _____

Total number of new teachers: _____

Number of first-year teachers assigned a mentor teacher: _____

Number of newly hired experienced teachers assigned a mentor teacher:

_____

Percentage of all new hires assigned mentor teachers: _____ %

Number of trained mentors: _____

Number of untrained mentors: _____

Average number of "formal" meetings in a typical month between mentor and mentee: _____

Average number of hours in a typical month spent in both formal and informal meetings between mentor and mentee: _____

Amount budgeted for the mentoring program: $ _____

Other: _____

Now consider what all these numbers imply. (This process also touches on evaluating for improvement.)

1. Was the data available to answer all these questions? _____

   If not, why not? _____

2. If all newly hired teachers are not assigned mentors, why not?

   _____

3. Are experienced teachers who are new to your district mentored differently from beginning teachers? _____

4. If some mentors are untrained, why? _____

   _____

5. Are there more, less, or the exact number of trained mentors available to meet needs? _____

6. Is there a large disparity among mentor-mentee pairs in terms of the amount of time spent in mentoring? _____

7. Was the money budgeted for mentoring realistic in terms of people, time, services, and materials actually needed? _____

Initial Outcomes

An outcome is something that occurs the way it does because of the existence of the program. Outcomes described or implied in statements of purpose, goals, or objectives are desired and anticipated. Outcomes can also occur serendipitously. Such unanticipated outcomes may be positive or negative, and may well have as much importance as those that are planned. When we focus on outcomes, our attention shifts from, "Did we do what we were supposed to do?" to "Did it work?"

We know that the evaluation of outcomes really begins at the beginning—with the development of purpose, goals, and objectives—and continues during and after implementation of the program. In a new program, it is unlikely that there will be enough of such "during and after" data available to evaluate the lofty outcomes typical of most goals and objectives. We also know that "three to five years is not an unreasonable time span for a significant change to take place in schools" (Loucks-Horsley & Zacchei, 1983). Therefore, it is both realistic and prudent to develop goals and objectives that recognize the fact that change takes time.

I offer the following suggestion: Develop a five-year evaluation plan. The stated outcomes for the first year should focus more on the operation of the program than on the program's effects. Such a plan might, for example, state that *"in accordance with established criteria and in a timely manner, X number of mentors will have been selected, provided with appropriate training, and assigned to mentees."*

As you develop outcomes for the program's second, third, and fourth years, you can focus more and more on areas associated with goals and purpose: on such things, for example, as higher retention rates of new teachers; increased knowledge, skills, and strategies of both new and experienced teachers; increased collegiality and collaboration among faculty; and even improvement in student learning. By the fifth year, you will have tested (and perhaps modified) most outcomes, and will be ready to carry out a comprehensive, researched-based evaluation of the entire program. In order to do so, you will need to anticipate early on what baseline data you will need over time, and to collect systematically that data as they become available.

Exercise 7.2 Develop an Outcome Through the Process of Reflection

1. Think of a situation or condition you would like to result from your mentoring program—one that would require some sort of change to take place. Keep that situation or condition in mind while completing Items 2 through 8 of this exercise.

2. Project your thoughts into the future. Imagine that the desired outcome is already attained. Using the present tense, describe what you see, hear, and feel. What are others saying or doing? What are you saying or doing? _____

    _____

    _____

3. Describe your reason for wanting this outcome. How will teaching and learning in your school or district be better because of it?

    _____

    _____

    _____

4. Can the outcome you envision be measured in any way? When you projected your thoughts into the future, was there an observable change that had taken place? How were things different from the way they are now? _____

    _____

    _____

5. What is a realistic date or time line by which you can reasonably expect to achieve this outcome? _____

    _____

    _____

6. What are your chances of achieving this outcome? Assess your resources: Do you have or can you get enough of what it will take to achieve your outcome in the time you have allowed?

    *   Money? _____

    *   Materials and equipment? _____

    *   Help and support? _____

    *   Space? _____

    *   Time? _____

    *   Expertise? _____

    *   Commitment? _____

Exercise 7.2 (continued)

7. Can you honestly say that the outcome you envision is achievable and worthwhile? _____

   Earlier, in Chapter 6, we developed outcome statements in terms of professional development. As a reminder, here again are five indicators of a well-developed outcome:

   - It is measurable and observable.
   - It expresses what you really want and are willing to work for.
   - It has a reasonable time line and/or deadline.
   - It has access to the resources it needs in order to succeed.
   - Its achievement not only enhances teaching and learning, but is also a learning experience in itself.

8. Now, state your desired outcome. State it in the future perfect tense.

   _____

   _____

   _____

To illustrate, here is how I might follow Steps 1–8 in Exercise 7.2 to develop an outcome statement for the evaluation process.

1. I would like new teachers in my school/district to acquire the habit of keeping a journal in which they record and reflect on their practice, and to use the results of that reflection to modify their future actions.

2. Projecting into the future, I see new teachers writing in journals and discussing with their mentors their recent professional experiences, the results of those experiences, and the thoughts and feelings evoked by them. I listen to mentors using their mentoring skills to encourage their mentees to reflect on their experiences and make informed decisions about modifying their actions as a result. Peeking over the shoulder of a new teacher writing in her journal, I read, "I often find myself jumping in with the 'correct' answer instead of waiting for the kids to figure it out for themselves. I need to develop my teacher patience—my 'wait time'—and not see moments of silence as gaps in the conversation for me to fill, but rather as opportunities for students to comprehend, analyze, and construct."

3. To me, reflection is a type of learning process where the teacher and pupil are located in the same individual. As such, reflection can be a powerful stimulator of growth that can help new teachers progress through development from novice to master teacher. I also consider journal writing to be an important strategy for reflection.

4. The data needed to determine the extent to which new teachers have increased their use of reflection and made changes as a result might include interviews of both mentors and mentees, the administration of a satisfaction scale, and scanning samples of journal entries and lesson plans over time. Such data might describe, for example, changes in attitudes and opinions about journal writing and reflection, changes in frequency and quality of reflection, and specific changes made in actions and understandings as a direct result of reflection.

5. Developing the habits of journal writing and reflecting seems to be a reasonable expectation for new teachers during the first year of a program. By the end of the new teacher's second year, I would expect that modification of action as a result of reflecting on journal entries will have become a norm. Therefore, the achievement of this outcome can best be assessed at the end of year two.

6. Some, but no significant amounts of money or space would be involved in achieving this outcome. Expenses might include the purchase of logbooks and the production of survey instruments. Time would need to be available for reflection and mentor-mentee interaction. The mentors will need some expertise in the mechanics of journal writing and reflection, and both mentor and mentee will need to become comfortable with

and committed to the process. It is unrealistic, however, to expect *all* new teachers to achieve this outcome.

7. As a result of achieving this outcome, new teachers will become better teachers sooner than they might otherwise (a worthwhile objective, by the way, to evaluate at the end of year four or five).

8. Statement of outcome: By the end of their second full year of teaching, at least 75% of teachers who have participated as mentees in the mentoring program will have posted, at an average of twice a month, journal entries relevant to their professional experience, and will have demonstrated a minimum of two changes or modifications in their professional actions as the result of such reflections.

Evaluating for Purposes of Improvement

As you may have noticed, evaluation undertaken for purposes of accountability is descriptive. It delineates how things are now, perhaps how they have changed from the past, and possibly how they are expected to be in the future. As stated earlier, the purpose of evaluation for accountability is to provide evidence that will have bearing on decisions about the program's continued existence.

Evaluating for purposes of *improvement*, however, tends to be inferential. It involves what educators often refer to as formative evaluation. It looks at ways the various components of a program are being carried out, whether the ways they are being carried out are resulting in desired outcomes, and to what extent the components themselves are proving to be appropriate. It also attempts to capture and understand unexpected outcomes. Results are used to fine-tune or modify aspects of the program to make them more effective.

Consider the case of School District X. District X was expecting to hire an exceptionally large number of teachers over the next few years, and consequently decided to develop a mentoring program for new teachers. A planning task group was formed, which developed, proposed to the school board, and received approval for a four-year pilot program. The program would be evaluated for improvement at the end of its first and second years, and at the end of years three and four for accountability.

As planned, the first year was devoted to start-up. No actual mentoring took place; rather, a representative committee was formed, policies and procedure were developed, and mentor teachers were selected and trained. Among the policies adapted was one requiring mentors to document the date, time, and duration of their meetings with mentees, and to submit that information to the mentees' principals along with brief descriptions of the purpose and results of the meetings. Mentors were selected in December, and trained during winter vacation in February, for which they received a generous stipend. By the beginning of March, start-up was completed, and the committee felt confident that everything was ready to go. In accordance with the program's criteria, the new mentors were matched with new teachers at the start of the next school year and provided with additional time during the school year to carry out their roles.

Committee members assumed that they had planned well and that, in the words of the chairperson, "things were going just fine, thank you very much." When evaluation for improvement was carried out at the end of the first year of operation, they were surprised by several findings.

- Mentors doubted their effectiveness in carrying out their responsibilities, citing confusion as to what those responsibilities actually were.

- Mentors expressed a lack of confidence in their ability to translate the mentoring theory they had learned in training into actual practice. Given the lapse of several months between training and its actual application, mentors felt they had forgotten some of the finer points they had learned about the skills of mentoring.

- New teachers were disappointed by what they saw as the propensity of their mentors to expect them to do everything the same way the mentors did. They felt as though they were being treated like graduate students rather than colleagues and were not trusted to make their own decisions.

- New teachers were concerned that by filing reports with principals about their meetings, mentors were in effect participating in their formal evaluation. Therefore, they were reluctant to divulge to their mentors any problems they might be having in the classroom.

Exercise 7.3 *Respond to Areas of Concern*

Suppose you were a member of the District X mentoring committee: What might you do to respond to the areas of concern expressed by mentors and mentees in the above scenario? I'll let you know in the next section what the District X committee did, but, first, write your thoughts below or on a separate sheet of paper.

_____

_____

_____

_____

_____

Now, here is what the District X mentoring committee did. Realizing that too much time had elapsed between mentor training and its application, and that there had been no opportunity for mentors to share and receive feedback once the school year began, the committee scheduled training for the next cohort of mentors to take place in late summer and added three additional sessions with the trainer during the school year. The first cohort of mentors was invited to attended. The committee also assembled a collection of professional books, periodicals, and other materials for both mentors and beginning teachers. In order to clarify roles, responsibilities, and expectations at the beginning of the next year, mentors and mentees, along with a facilitator, met together for a full day during the orientation week for new teachers. As for the issue of submitting documentation of mentor-mentee meetings to the principal, the policy was changed (with approval of the teachers union representative who had opposed the original policy) to require a recording of meeting times and dates *only*—not anything else. It was made clear that this was solely for purposes of accountability, because mentors were to receive stipends.

Collecting Data to Evaluate for Improvement

As mentioned earlier, data collected for purposes of accountability can also suggest areas needing improvement. For example, demographics showing that a program will have too few trained mentors for the number of expected new teachers indicate a need to make some adjustments in your recruiting, selecting, compensating, and/or mentor-mentee matching policies and procedures.

It is this informal, open-ended kind of data gathering, however, that brings to the surface the unexpected happenings and subtle nuances that are a program's pressure points, those easily overlooked places where things are not what they had seemed at first blush. For example, in the District X scenario above, the mentees' feelings about the required submission of meeting reports and the effect those feelings had on the mentor-mentee relationship would have been unlikely to have surfaced during the collection of data for accountability.

So how does one go about gathering information for purposes of improving a program? In the late 1970s, Professors James McKenney of Harvard University and Peter Keen of Stanford University suggested that people function predominantly in one of two contrasting mind sets when it comes to gathering information: preceptive and receptive. In an article describing the work of McKenney and Keen, author David Ewing (1977) refers to Sherlock Holmes as an example of a receptive information gatherer. Holmes, writes Ewing,

> is always at odds with the preceptive styles of Dr. Watson and the detectives at Scotland Yard, who zero in on the "obvious" suspect, and fit the facts to build a case against him. Holmes is titillated by

odd and assorted facts, and on the basis of trifling details, uncovers more leads and finally builds a hypothesis that leads to the murderer.

When gathering information for purposes of program improvement, don your double-visored Sherlock Holmes cap and activate your receptive information-gathering persona. Focus on details. Digest and ponder individual facts and clues without trying to fit them into any preconceived conceptual scheme. Be aware of the feel and inherent qualities of new information. Suspend judgment. Save your Dr. Watson style for accountability-focused evaluations.

Structured interviews, observations, and surveys are the most common data-gathering methods used for evaluation. Here are a few additional ways to elicit information, especially when evaluating for improvement. These open-ended methods may well provide unanticipated information that may not otherwise come to your attention.

- Read journal entries.

- Arrange storytelling and experience-sharing sessions among small groups of mentors and/or mentees.

- Hold discussions around a specific aspect of the program, such as the nature of various people's perceptions of roles and responsibilities in the program, including one's own.

- Ask people to answer an open-ended set of questions on a topic such as the value and downside of having been a mentor (or mentee) during the past year.

- Seek perceptions of those not directly involved with the program.

- Administer an end-of-year questionnaire to mentors and mentees, comparing what each group perceives with what the other considers to be the most and least successful results of the mentoring process.

- Ask for feedback from teachers who have left the school or district. The Rochester (New York) City School District, for example, has identified over the years several areas needing improvement in its mentoring program by means of an "exit survey." The instrument asks for a person's reason for leaving, positive and negative experiences on the job, and feelings about the district that may have contributed to the decision to leave. The survey also asks for information and suggestions to help the district retain teachers in the future.

I'll leave you with Michael Q. Patton's challenge (1980) regarding evaluation: "[Get] the best possible information to the people who need it—and then [get] those people to actually use the information in appropriate ways for intended purposes."

8

Some Other Programs Related to Mentoring

Sir Edward Fritillary was a renowned lepidopterist. He traveled all over the world collecting rare and beautiful butterflies using a butterfly net he designed himself. One day, a friend invited Sir Edward to go on a hunting safari in Africa. The friend, an experienced big game hunter, suggested several models of rifles for Sir Edward to consider purchasing for the hunt. Sir Edward ignored the suggestions; he knew how to capture his prey. When the renegade bull elephant charged, Sir Edward faced it head on. Unfortunately, Sir Edward's butterfly net was not quite the correct implement for this situation. Sir Edward's son, Harry, inherited his father's butterfly collection.

What does this little fable have to do with mentoring programs? It suggests that there may be other ways to get the job done.

Three recently developed models are expanding the concept of mentoring beyond the traditional "experienced teacher helping to induct the novice teacher into the profession" mentoring model. They are

1. Support and learning groups for new teachers

2. Co-mentoring between and among experienced peers

3. Peer assistance and review for teachers who receive unsatisfactory evaluations

Support and Learning Groups for New Teachers

Although pairing every novice with a trained teacher-mentor is fundamental to a viable mentoring program, new teachers also need to have opportunities to meet regularly in a "user-friendly" group environment where they can interact with each other. For example, Professors Dwight

L. Rogers and Leslie Babinsky (1999) at the University of North Carolina at Chapel Hill School of Education have created new teacher groups "to offer a safe place where beginning teachers can voice their concerns, share their joys and frustrations, and help one another deal with problems. Establishing regularly scheduled times . . . also gives them the chance to learn and grow professionally."

Several school districts, in addition to providing one-on-one support from mentors, also provide regularly scheduled group sessions for their new teachers. Here are a few examples.

- *Pittsburgh, PA:* On a monthly basis throughout the school year, new teachers attend sessions that focus on such topics as what to do during the first three weeks of school, and how to maintain an orderly classroom. At each of these sessions, teachers also meet in various grade-level teams led by a mentor teacher from the same level. This arrangement was developed by a collaborative arrangement between the Pittsburgh Federation of Teachers and the school district.

- *Kenosha, WI:* The district requires teachers having fewer than two years of teaching experience to attend nine monthly seminars related to district initiatives and the needs of beginning teachers. Small-group support sessions are also provided.

- *Baldwin Park Unified Schools, Los Angeles County, CA:* The program runs an annual "New Teacher Academy," a voluntary week-long series of intensive training sessions for first-year teachers.

- *Minneapolis, MN:* The district's negotiated contract contains sections on "Staff Development for New Teachers" and "Professional Support for New Teachers." These sections incorporate such provisions as the following:

    Teachers during their first year of employment or reemployment . . . are required to attend . . . ten (10) inservice meetings. The agenda will be established through a collaborative process . . . [New teachers will] attend the Professional Support Process in September . . . This session will include: Setting Professional Support Goals . . . [and] Learning about the role of the Professional Portfolio as a tool for growth and for documenting progress.

- *Baltimore, MD:* In addition to a mandatory five-day orientation in August, the district offers an optional month-long summer program for its new teachers. Participants receive stipends, and have the opportunity to prepare for the classroom and become familiar with the state's education standards. New teachers opting for the program also learn, for example, how to conduct parent-teacher conferences and student assessment strategies.

Some state departments of education provide professional development activities for new teachers geared specifically toward meeting the challenges particular to early career teaching. For example,

- Massachusetts, during the spring of 2000, piloted Case Study Seminars for beginning teachers at several sites within the state. The five 3-hour sessions provided participants "from across the teaching disciplines with support that is relevant to their current classroom experience, and the opportunity to collaborate with other beginning teachers from a variety of districts."

- Connecticut provides between 18 and 20 hour-long Content-Focused Support Seminars for its beginning teachers, which

  > are designed to provide specific professional development to beginning teachers participating in the portfolio assessment process . . . [leading them] through a series of explorations about effective teaching practices within their disciplines and the relationship of the professional teaching standards to the specific context of their teaching.

Co-Mentoring

"It is odd, " write Barbara Frase and Michael McAsey in "Peer Visits: How to Start Productive Conversations on Teaching" (1998), "that our professional community is simultaneously open and insular."

> Outside of the classroom we speak openly with our colleagues about serious matters, yet there are colleagues we have known for years whose classroom persona we don't know at all. We suffer a diminished sense of community and lose a precious opportunity for renewed vigor in our teaching as a result of this insularity. Our peers are often our most valued font of encouragement as well as rich sources of information and ideas . . . more [so] than almost any other professional interaction.

The most prevalent, and probably oldest application of co-mentoring is what is commonly called *peer coaching*. Typically, peer coaching is when experienced faculty observe each other's teaching styles and discuss effective teaching methods. It is important to point out that in the peer-coaching model, classroom visits are not evaluation visits; rather, they are developmental processes providing data and diagnostic and descriptive feedback. By participating in peer-coaching dyads or groups—whose sole purpose is to mutually enhance teaching and learning effectiveness—veteran teachers can break the isolation of the classroom and look at their practices through safe, objective and friendly eyes.

Carol A. Mullen of the University of South Florida College of Education describes another form of co-mentoring in which "different professionals across a school-university setting come together to form a new culture of learning . . . [where] teachers, administrators, and professors can learn from synergistic relations with one another." Professor Mullen (2000) observes that

> university faculty are grounded in theory while school faculty are grounded in practice, but neither group has established a process with which to mentor one another and to become co-researchers and co-authors. The solution . . . [is to] enroll both groups to serve as mentors for one another. This collaborative framework provided the guidance necessary to . . . integrate theory and practice.

Peer Assistance and Review

When powerful national education organizations create new policies or modify existing ones, the effect on local programs can be profound. Such was the case when on September 25–27, 1998, the NEA and AFT joined together in Washington, D.C., for a Conference on Teacher Quality. At that conference, the AFT and NEA introduced their jointly published handbook, *Peer Assistance and Peer Review*. The Introduction to the AFT/NEA handbook distinguishes between peer assistance and peer review, explaining that they are actually two distinct activities:

> *Peer Assistance* aims to help new and veteran teachers improve their knowledge and skills. Such a program links new teachers— or struggling veteran teachers—with consulting teachers who provide ongoing support through observing, modeling, sharing ideas and skills and recommending materials for further study.

Peer assistance thus is very much akin to mentoring.

The handbook goes on to say that *"Peer Review* adds one significant element to peer assistance—the consulting teachers conduct formal evaluations and make recommendations regarding the continued employment of participating teachers." Peer review can profoundly alter a local mentoring program because the concept attacks one of the basic tenets of the mentor-mentee relationship: the separation of mentoring from evaluation.

From my personal point of view, a Peer Assistance and Review (PAR) program is not mentoring, nor should it be considered mentoring: It is supervision and evaluation. Trust and confidentiality are vital components of mentoring. It is virtually impossible for anyone—especially a new teacher in a new environment trying to prove himself or herself—to expose insecurities and inexperience to a coworker, and to leave himself or herself vulnerable to possible ridicule and censure. Yet it may be necessary for a mentee to risk these behaviors in order to help the mentor understand the crux of a situation. This degree of openness may be difficult to achieve if it is the mentor's responsibility to evaluate the mentee or to recommend certification. The peer mentor and the peer reviewer must be different people.

Such is the case, for example, in Connecticut's PAR-like Beginning Educator Support and Training (BEST) program, which is a primary reason the program works so well. The trained mentor's role in the BEST program is to help the mentee prepare for review, not to be part of it. The reviewer or evaluator is an entirely different person, generally from a different school district, who has been trained for that altogether different role.

Because the NEA and AFT together represent the vast majority of public school teachers in the United States, their policies deeply influence day-to-day operations in the nation's public schools. The new teacher induction and peer review policies adopted by both organizations and advocated in the PAR Handbook are no exceptions. Consequently, it is not surprising that some districts are developing PAR programs.

It is prudent for districts considering instituting a PAR program not only to do so in collaboration with the local teachers union, but also, as the AFT/NEA handbook points out, to decide (a) to what extent the program will entail formal evaluation by peers, and (b) which teachers the program will serve. Will it serve all new teachers, only new teachers with problems, or veteran teachers identified as needing remediation?

Some districts instituted peer assistance and peer review well before its endorsement by the teacher unions, the first being Toledo in 1981. Toledo's program, as is the case with most that followed, provided PAR both to new teachers *and* to veteran teachers who were experiencing difficulties in the classroom. As of this writing, several medium and large cities, including Boston, Cincinnati, Milwaukee, Minneapolis, New York City, and Rochester, have joined Toledo in instituting PAR, but no state has mandated it. However, California, for one, has allocated substantial financial incentives for districts to establish PAR programs, and over 500 of the state's districts have applied for the increased funding—which in the case of the Los Angeles Unified School District, for example, would mean more than $4.5 million in additional state aid.

Reviews of the effectiveness of PAR and how it has been received by the education community are mixed. For instance, according to the Ohio State Department of Education, the Columbus Public School District has a lower rate of attrition than similar districts because of PAR, and the Ohio DOE awarded Columbus's PAR program its Distinguished Award for Excellence in Staff Development. California's Poway Unified School District's PAR program has been in existence since 1987. Teachers and administrators are in agreement that the program has given new teachers much-welcomed help and removed some teachers who "belonged in another profession."

Among the most vocal critics of PAR is former labor negotiator Myron Lieberman. In his 1998 book *Teachers Evaluating Teachers: Peer Review and the New Unionism*, Lieberman contends that teacher evaluation is the province of administrators, and that teachers are placed in the awkward position of judging their colleagues down the hall who are teaching the same students they teach. Another critic of the process is a teacher with whom I recently had a conversation about peer review. He argued that "when your colleague steps into your classroom to 'review' you, he or she is no longer your peer. Rather, the relationship between you has fundamentally changed."

As you might imagine, the decision whether or not to buy into the PAR concept has elicited much reflection and discussion. If it has not already done so, your school or district may have to address this issue. If you do decide to become a PAR district, will the program entail peer assistance as well as peer review? Looking at the adoption of peer assistance and review with a systems mind-set, potentially profound changes in an existing program will be inevitable.

There may some aspect in each of the three models described above that can be applied to your program. It would certainly be worth your committee's time to consider the potential.

Inventing the Future
Planning an Exemplary Program

The mentoring committee's first official act was to elect Gloria Billingham as its chair. Gloria accepted the honor, took a deep breath, and murmured a brief, silent prayer: "Please help me get this potentially great committee off to a great start."

Indeed, the newly formed committee was potentially great. Members represented all the groups and organizations in the district that had a stake in the development and success of a mentoring program for new teachers. Not only that—every member was an enthusiastic volunteer, and had agreed to participate actively in the committee's work.

The committee's second act was to agree on its goal: *to plan, implement, and nurture an exemplary mentoring program.* Operationally, this meant that the committee would need to decide what aspects of mentoring it would address; what standards would apply to each aspect; what activities and resources would be involved in implementing each aspect; what the time line for developing and implementing each aspect would be; and who would be responsible for seeing to the development, implementation and efficacy of each aspect of the plan.

The remainder of the meeting was devoted to a general discussion of mentoring, during which it was agreed to devote a full year to planning for the achievement of the committee's goal. A set of relevant reference materials was distributed, the discussion of which was to be the major agenda item for the next meting.

Turn Meeting Hours Into Action Minutes

Gloria's committee spent a great deal of its meeting time making decisions. The committee's secretary used the organizer, *Action Minutes* (see Exercise 9.1), to record decisions made and actions planned. You are welcome to adopt or adapt it for your own use.

Action Minutes

Page _____ of _____

Members Present _____

_____ **Today's Date** _____

_____ **Recorder** _____

_____ **Next Meeting** _____

Agenda Item	Initiated by	Summary of Discussion	Decision (action/task)	Responsibility	Target Date

Possible Agenda for Next Meeting:

Notes:

Consider the Possibilities

One month and two meetings later, Gloria leaned back and glanced around the room. For the past 90 minutes, the now empty meeting place had buzzed with activity. Newsprint covered with red, blue, and black marker ink lined the back wall, and echoes of heated discussion still bounced from the others. Gloria reflected for a moment on what the mentoring committee had accomplished during its brief existence. "Yes," she concluded, "my prayer has been answered. The committee has gotten off to a great start."

She looked at the last sheet of newsprint, the one that summarized the results of the committee's brainstorming that covered all the other sheets. The word *Components* was on top of the sheet—underlined in red. The rest of the page, a 10-item bulleted list, was neatly printed in black. These were the components the committee decided to include in their district's mentoring program:

- Time
- Budget
- Compensation
- Selection of mentors
- Mentor training
- Selection of mentees
- Matching mentors and mentees
- Professional development
- Program evaluation
- Coordination and oversight

In order to apply a systems mind-set to the decision process, the committee had subjected each component under consideration to an examination using the criteria introduced at the beginning of Chapter 5. Again, these criteria are as follows:

1. Why are we making this decision?
2. What could happen if we don't make this decision?
3. What, if anything, will be better because of this decision?
4. What, if anything, will be worse because of this decision?
5. What effect, if any, will making this decision have on people?
6. What effect, if any, will making this decision have on other elements of the mentoring program?

7. What effect, if any, will making this decision have on the school's or district's macrosystems?

8. Will it work in the context of the school's or district's policies, budget, and operational structure?

9. Will it work in the context of the school's or district's informal culture?

10. Will it work in the context of the school's or district's professional contracts and agreements?

Gloria recalled how two potential components—peer review and mentoring administrators—were rejected as a result of applying this process.

The agenda for the next meeting consisted of one item: Develop an action plan. The 90-minute meeting seemed to fly by, so animated and focused was the discussion. Again, after everyone had left the meeting room, Gloria sat back and murmured her little thank-you prayer. She looked at the sheets of newsprint that this meeting had generated. As before, a single sheet at the end of the row summarized the words and phrases that filled all the others. The summary sheet listed five considerations that each component of the new mentoring program would receive during the planning phase:

- Standards: the desired attributes of the component expressed in observable and measurable terms

- Resources: the time, materials, equipment, funding, and people needed to implement and support the component

- Due Date: the target date for having the component ready for implementation

- Responsibility: the person (probably a committee member) who will "honcho" or lead the planning effort for the component

- Notes: a "To-Do" and "Reminder" list of tasks and activities related to the implementation of the component

Organize Your Plan

Gloria fashioned the two lists—components and considerations—into the planning organizer in Exercise 9.2.

You may find it useful to prepare an enlarged version of this planning organizer for your own committee's use. You are welcome to change items to match your district's criteria.

Exercise 9.2 Mentoring Program Planning Organizer

Mentoring Program Planning Organizer

Conditions / Components	Standards	Resources	Due Date	Responsibility	Notes
Time					
Budget					
Compensation					
Mentor Selection					
Mentee Selection					
Mentor Training					
Matching Mentors & Mentees					
Professional Development					
Program Evaluation					
Coordination and Oversight					

Figure 9.1 Planning for Mentor Training

Standards	Resources	Due Date	Responsibility	Notes
• Twelve K-5 mentors trained for elementary school, 5 for middle school, 5 for high school—subject areas and building to match that of new teachers • Training 4 days in August, followed by 2-hour sessions every other week during September and October and a 2-hour session once a month, November through May • Content includes developing relationships, assessing mentee needs and styles, classroom observation and coaching skills, classroom management, lesson planning, and subject-specific strategies	• Competent, experienced trainers • Off-site facilities in August; on-site facilities during school year • Training materials and equipment • Budget: facilities & food, $4000; stipends, $22,000; Trainers, $10,000; travel, $1,000; substitutes, $2,000; publications, printing, consumable materials, misc., $4000—total $43,000	• June 30	• Fred K. (committee member) in cooperation with chair of professional development committee and mentoring program coordinator	• Apply for state grant • Clear schedule on school calendar • Commitment from mentors to participate (college credit?) • Any curriculum revisions lately? • Contract with trainer(s) • Check training content against state guidelines • Reserve training sites and arrange for food • Inform teachers union and school board of plans

Figure 9.1 is an example of how Gloria's committee used the Program Planning Organizer to plan one of the components—Mentor Training.

Planning Progress Checklist

Gloria and the committee developed the following checklist to help keep track of their progress. The brief list was posted on the wall of the committee's meeting room next to the Mentoring Program Planning Organizer, and each item was crossed off as it was accomplished. As was the case with Gloria's committee, your planning group may find the use of such a device both helpful and motivating.

1. Due dates for having program components ready for implementation:

   Time   Date _____

   Budget   Date _____

   Compensation   Date _____

   Selection of mentors   Date _____

   Selection of mentees   Date _____

   Mentor training   Date _____

   Matching mentors and mentees Date _____

   Professional development   Date _____

   Program evaluation   Date _____

   Coordination and oversight   Date _____

2. Periodically inform school/district community of progress (elicit feedback):

   Date _____   Method _____

   Date _____   Method _____

   Date _____   Method _____

   Date _____   Method _____

3. Program implemented! _____

Resource A
Professional Associations

AACTE
American Associate of Colleges for Teacher Education
1307 New York Ave., S.W., Suite 300
Washington, DC 20005-4701
Phone: 202/293-2450
http://www.aacte.org

AASA
American Association of School Administrators
1801 North Moore Street
Arlington, VA 22209-1813
Phone: 703/528-0700
http://www.aasa.org

AERA
The American Educational Research Association
1230 17th Street NW
Washington, DC 20036
Phone: 202/223-9485
http://www.aera.net

AFT
American Federation of Teachers
555 New Jersey Avenue, NW
Washington, DC 20001
Phone: 202/879-4400
http://www.aft.org

ASCD
The Association for Supervision and Curriculum Development
1703 North Beauregard Street
Alexandria, VA 22311-1714
Phone: 703/578-9600 or 800/933-ASCD
http://www.ascd.org

IMA
International Mentoring Association
Western Michigan University
Conferences and Seminars
1201 Oliver Street
Kalamazoo, MI 49008-5161
Phone: 616/387-4174
http://www.wmich.edu/conferences/mentoring

NAESP
The National Association of Elementary School Principals
1615 Duke Street
Alexandria, VA 22314
Phone: 800/386-2377 or 703/684-3345
http://www.naesp.org

NASSP
National Association of Secondary School Principals
1904 Association Drive
Reston, VA 20191-1537
Phone: 703/860-0200
http://www.nassp.org

NEA
National Education Association
1201 16th Street
Washington, DC 20036
Phone: 202/833-4000
http://www.nea.org

NSDC
National Staff Development Council
PO Box 240
Oxford, OH 45056
Phone: 513/523-6029
http://www.nsdc.org

PDK
Phi Delta Kappa International
408 N. Union St., P.O. Box 789
Bloomington, IN 47402-0789
Phone: 812/339-1156 or 800/766-1156
http://www.pdkintl.org

References

American Federation of Teachers. (1998, September). *Educational issues policy brief* (No. 5). American Federation of Teachers: Author.

American Federation of Teachers and National Education Association. (1998). *Peer assistance and peer review.* Handbook prepared for the AFT/NEA Conference on Teacher Quality. Washington, DC: Author.

Brock, B. L. (1998). *Standardizing the mentorship program.* Paper presented at the annual meeting of the Mid-Western Educational Research Association, Chicago.

Clinton, W. J. (1997). *Call to action for American education in the 21st century.* From the president's State of the Union address, February 4, 1997.

Darling-Hammond, L. (1999). *Solving the dilemmas of teacher supply, demands and standards.* Report for the National Commission on Teaching and America's Future. New York: Columbia University Teachers College.

Evans, W., Honemann, D., & Bolch, T. (Eds.). (2000). *Roberts rules of Order.* New York: Perseus Book Group.

Ewing, D. (1977, December). Discovering your problem-solving style. *Psychology Today,* vol. 11, pp. 68-70ff.

Frase, B., & McAsey, M. (1998, March). Peer visits: How to start productive conversations on teaching. *National Teaching and Learning Forum,* pp. 1-3.

Gillespie, R. J. (1972). A creative approach to evaluating ideas. In A. M. Biondi (Ed.), *The creative process* (pp. 54-61). Buffalo, NY: D.O.K. Publishers.

Good morning, America. (1999, January 15). Produced by Melissa Dunst, ABC Network.

Herman, J. L., & Fitz-Gibbon, C. (1987). *Evaluator's handbook.* Newbury Park, CA: Sage.

Janas, M. (1996, Fall). Mentoring the mentor. *Journal of Staff Development, 17*(4), 2-5.

Janis, I. L. (1972). *Victims of groupthink.* New York: Houghton Mifflin.

Leedy, P. D., & Ormrod, J. E. (2001). *Practical research* (7th ed.). Upper Saddle River, NJ: Prentice-Hall.

Lieberman, M. (1998). *Teachers evaluating teachers: Peer review and the new unionism.* Washington, DC: Education Policy Institute.

Little, J. W. (1993, Summer). Teachers' professional development in a climate of educational reform. *Educational Evaluation and Policy Analysis, 15*(2), 129-151.

Loucks-Horsley, S., & Zacchei, D. (1983, November). Applying our findings to today's innovations. *Educational Leadership,* pp. 28-31.

Maslow, A. H. (1954). *Motivation and personality.* New York: Harper & Row.

Mullen, C. A. (2000, Winter). Constructing co-mentoring partnerships: Walkways we must travel. *Theory Into Practice,* pp. 4-11.

National Center for Education Statistics. (1999, January). *Teacher quality* (Report). Washington, DC: U.S. Department of Education.

National Foundation for the Improvement of Education. (1999). *Creating a teacher mentoring program.* Report based on the proceedings of the Nation Foundation for the Improvement of Education Teacher Mentoring Symposium, Los Angeles. National Foundation for the Improvement of Education: Author.

Newton, A., Bergstrom, K., Brennan, N., Dunne, K., Gilbert, C., Ibarguen, N., Perez-Selles, M., & Thomas, E. (1994). *Mentoring: A resource and training guide for educators.* Andover, MA: The Regional Laboratory for Educational Improvement of the Northeast and Islands.

Patton, M. Q. (1980). *Qualitative evaluational methods.* Beverly Hills, CA: Sage.

Portner, H. (1998). *Mentoring new teachers.* Thousand Oaks, CA: Corwin.

Raywid, M. A. (1993, September). Finding time for collaboration. *Educational Leadership,* pp. 30-34.

Regan, H., Dubea, C., Anceil, M., Vailancourt, R., & Hofmann, J. (1992). *Teacher—A new definition and model for development and evaluation.* Philadelphia: Research for Better Schools.

Regulations for the certification of educational personnel in Massachusetts. Massachusetts General Laws, Chapter 71, Sec. 38G, 603. Commonwealth of Massachusetts Regulations 7.00.

Rogers, D. L., & Babinsky, L. (1999, May). Breaking through isolation with new teacher groups. *Educational Leadership,* pp. 38-40.

Rowley, J. B. (1999, May). The good mentor. *Educational Leadership,* pp. 20-22.

Rowley, J., & Hart, P. (2000a). *Facilitator's guide to high performance mentoring.* Thousand Oaks, CA: Corwin.

Rowley, J., & Hart, P. (2000b). *High performance mentoring.* Thousand Oaks, CA: Corwin.

Saphier, J., & Gower, R. (1997). *The skillful teacher.* Carlisle, MA: Research for Better Teaching.

Sweeney, B., & Johnson, T. (1999). *Mentoring to improve schools.* Alexandria, VA: Association for Supervision and Curriculum Development.

U.S. Department of Education. (1997, July). *Seven priorities of the U.S. Department of Education.* Washington, DC: Author.

U.S. News & World Report. (1999, January 18). *Seasoned Teachers, 125*(2), 56.

Wong, H., & Wong, R. (2000, July). Effective teaching. *Teacher Net Gazette.* Available on-line at HTTP://Teachers.net/gazette/Jul00/Wong.html

**CORWIN
PRESS**

The Corwin Press logo—a raven striding across an open book—represents the happy union of courage and learning. We are a professional-level publisher of books and journals for K–12 educators, and we are committed to creating and providing resources that embody these qualities. Corwin's motto is "Success for All Learners."